A RITUAL
FOR
LAYPERSONS

Rites for Holy Communion
and the
Pastoral Care of the Sick and Dying

A Liturgical Press Book

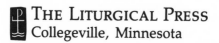

THE LITURGICAL PRESS
Collegeville, Minnesota

Concordat cum originali: Ronald F. Krisman
Executive Director
Secretariat for the Liturgy
National Conference of Catholic Bishops

Published by authority of the Bishops' Committee on the Liturgy, National Conference of Catholic Bishops

ACKNOWLEDGMENTS

Excerpts from the English translation of *Holy Communion and Worship of the Eucharist outside Mass* © 1974, International Committee on English in the Liturgy, Inc. (ICEL); excerpts from the English translation of *Pastoral Care of the Sick: Rites of Anointing and Viaticum* © 1982, ICEL; excerpts from the *Order of Christian Funerals* © 1985, ICEL. All rights reserved.

Scriptures are taken from the *New American Bible With Revised New Testament* Copyright © 1986 by the Confraternity of Christian Doctrine, 3211 Fourth Street, N.E., Washington, D.C. 20017-1194 and are used with permission. All rights reserved.

Scriptures are taken from the *Revised Psalms* Copyright © 1991 by the Confraternity of Christian Doctrine, 3211 Fourth Street, N.E., Washington, D.C. 20017-1194 and are used with permission. All rights reserved.

Cover design by Ann Blattner.

Printed in the United States of America.

ISBN 0-8146-2150-3

CONTENTS

PART IV
A SELECTION OF READINGS, RESPONSES,
AND VERSES FROM SACRED SCRIPTURE

PART V
PRAYERS FOR THE DEAD AND MOURNERS

Introduction

One of the unique features of the revised liturgical books published after the Second Vatican Council is the provision of certain rites at which a layperson is able to preside in the absence of a priest or deacon. This book gathers in one place such rites excerpted from: *Holy Communion and Worship of the Eucharist outside Mass, Pastoral Care of the Sick: Rites of Anointing and Viaticum,* and *Order of Christian Funerals.* Each of the ritual books contains rites for use by priests and deacons, as well as specific forms adapted for use by a minister who is a layperson.

Part I of this book provides lay ministers with the rite for holy communion outside Mass (Chapter 1). This rite is intended for use in a church, a chapel, or another suitable place when communion is distributed apart from Mass. The minister of the rite is an instituted acolyte or a special (extraordinary) minister of holy communion who has been so designated by the bishop and appointed to lead this service by the pastor. It is not intended for use on Sundays when no priest is available for the celebration of Mass, since liturgical provisions have been made for such circumstances in *Sunday Celebrations in the Absence of a Priest: Leader's Edition.*

Chapter 2 contains the rites for communion of the sick and viaticum, that is, holy communion for the dying. Persons who will bring communion to the sick should be specially trained for this ministry and are to be designated as special ministers of holy communion by the bishop and carry out their ministry under the direction of the pastor. In most cases, viaticum will be given by a priest or deacon, but there are circumstances when this responsibility may fall to a layperson.

Part II contains excerpts from *Pastoral Care of the Sick* and provides prayers and Scripture readings for use with an adult (Chapter 3) or a child (Chapter 4) who is sick. Laypersons who, as a part of a parish's total ministry to the sick, visit the sick may appropriately use these texts. Those who visit the sick need no special authorization of the bishop, but should be carefully prepared for this pastoral ministry and carry it out under the supervision of the pastor, who has the ultimate responsibility for the pastoral care of all the members of the parish who are sick.

Prayers and Scripture readings for the dying and for mourners are given in Part III: Pastoral Care of the Dying. Chapter 5 contains the Scripture readings and prayers for use with a dying person which have been taken from *Pastoral Care of the Sick.* This chapter also contains prayers for use with the family immediately after death while all are still gathered around the body. Because of the special needs of the dying and their families, laypersons who will visit them and are to use the rites provided here should be given adequate preparation for this ministry by the pastor.

Chapter 6 is taken from the *Order of Christian Funerals* and provides a brief order of prayer for use on the occasion of a lay minister's first visit or meeting with the family of the deceased following death.

Part IV presents a broad selection of Scripture readings and psalms for use in the celebration of the various rites contained in this book.

Part V contains a collection of prayers for the dead and for mourners adapted to a variety of circumstances.

It is hoped that this book will make several of the rites of the Church more accessible to laypersons who exercise the responsibility of pastoral care. The compilation obviates the need to go to a number of liturgical books and wade through a vast amount of rubrical material in order to determine which adaptations are to be made in each rite when led by a properly instructed and designated layperson.

Part I
HOLY COMMUNION
OUTSIDE MASS

Chapter 1

HOLY COMMUNION OUTSIDE MASS

INTRODUCTION

I. The Relationship between Communion Outside Mass and the Sacrifice

1   Sacramental communion received during Mass is a more complete participation in the eucharistic celebration. This truth stands out more clearly, by force of the sign value, when after the priest's communion the faithful receive the Lord's body and blood from the same sacrifice.[1] Therefore, recently baked bread should ordinarily be consecrated in every eucharistic celebration for the communion of the faithful.

2   The faithful are to be led to the practice of receiving communion during the actual eucharist celebration.

Priests, however, are not to refuse to give communion to the faithful who for a legitimate reason ask for it even outside Mass.[2]

In fact it is proper that those who are prevented from being present at the community's celebration should be refreshed with the eucharist. In this way they may realize that they are united not only with the Lord's sacrifice but also with the community itself and are supported by the love of their brothers and sisters.

Pastors should take care that the sick and the elderly be given the opportunity even if they are not gravely ill or in imminent danger of death, to receive the eucharist often, even

[1] See *SC* art. 55 [*DOL* 1, no. 55].
[2] See *SCR*, Instr. EuchMyst no. 33 a [*DOL* 179, no. 1262].

3

daily, especially during the Easter season. It is lawful to minister communion under the form of wine to those who cannot receive the consecrated bread.[3]

3   The faithful should be instructed carefully that, even when they receive communion outside Mass, they are closely united with the sacrifice that perpetuates the sacrfice of the cross. They are sharers in the sacred banquet in which "through the communion of the body and blood of the Lord, the people of God share the benefits of the paschal sacrifice, renew the new covenant with us made once and for all by God in Christ's blood, and in faith and hope foreshadow and anticipate the eschatological banquet in the Father's kingdom, as they proclaim the death of the Lord, until he comes."[4]

II. The Time of Communion Outside Mass

4   Communion may be given outside Mass on any day and at any hour. It is proper, however, to schedule the hours for giving communion, with a view to the convenience of the faithful, so that the celebration may take place in a fuller form and with greater spiritual benefit. Nevertheless:

a) On Holy Thursday communion may be given only during Mass; communion may be brought to the sick at any hour of the day.

b) On Good Friday communion may be given only during the celebration of the passion of the Lord; communion may be brought at any hour of the day to the sick who cannot participate in the celebration.

c) On Holy Saturday communion may be given only as viaticum.[5]

---

[3] See *ibid.*, nos. 40–41 [*DOL* 179, no. 1269–1270].

[4] *Ibid.*, no. 3 a [*DOL* 179, no. 1232].

[5] See *MR, Missa vespertina in Cena Domini,* 243; *Celebratio Passionis Domini* 250, no. 3; *Sabbato Sancto* 265 [*RM,* Holy Thursday, *Evening Mass of the Lord's Supper;* Good Friday, *Celebration of the Lord's Passion* no. 3; Holy Satuday].

III. THE MINISTER OF COMMUNION

5   It belongs first of all to the priest and the deacon to minister holy communion to the faithful who ask to receive it.[6] It is most fitting, therefore, that they give a suitable part of their time to this ministry of their order, depending on the needs of the faithful.

It also belongs to an acolyte who has been properly instituted to give communion as a special minister when the priest and deacon are absent or impeded by sickness, old age, or pastoral ministry or when the number of the faithful at the holy table is so great that the Mass or other service may be unreasonably prolonged.[7]

The local Ordinary may give other special ministers the faculty to give communion whenever it seems necessary for the pastoral benefit of the faithful and no priest, deacon, or acolyte is available.[8]

IV. THE PLACE OF COMMUNION OUTSIDE MASS

6   The place where communion outside Mass is ordinarily given is a church or oratory in which the eucharist is regularly celebrated or reserved, or a church, oratory, or other place where the local community regularly gathers for the liturgical assembly on Sundays or other days. Communion may be given, however, in other places, including private homes, when it is a question of the sick, prisoners, or others who cannot leave the place without danger or serious difficulty.

---

[6] See *SCR*, Instr. EuchMyst no. 31 [*DOL* 179, no. 1260].

[7] See Paul VI, Motu Proprio *Ministeria quaedam*, Aug. 15, 1972, no. VI [*DOL* 340, no. 2931].

[8] See *SCDS*, Instr. *Immensae caritatis*, January 29, 1973, 1, nos. I and II [*DOL* 264, nos. 2075–2076].

V. Regulations for Giving Communion

7   When communion is given in a church or oratory, a corporal is to be placed on the altar, which is already covered with a cloth, and there are to be two lighted candles as a sign of reverence and festiveness.[9] A communion plate is to be used.

When communion is given in other places, a suitable table is to be prepared and covered with a cloth; candles are also to be provided.

8   The minister of communion if he is a priest or deacon, is to be vested in an alb, or a surplice over a cassock, and a stole.

Other ministers should wear either the liturgical vesture that may be traditional in their region or attire that is in keeping with this ministry and has been approved by the Ordinary.

The eucharist for communion outside a church is to be carried in a pyx or other covered vessel; the vesture of the minister and the manner of carrying the eucharist should be appropriate and in accord with local circumstances.

9   In giving communion, the custom of placing the particle of consecrated bread on the tongue of the communicant is to be maintained because it is based on a tradition of several centuries.

Conferences of bishops, however, may decree, once their decision has been confirmed by the Apostolic See, the communion may also be given in their territories by placing the consecrated bread in the hand of the faithful, provided any danger is prevented of engendering in the attitudes of the faithful irreverence or false ideas about the eucharist.[10]

The faithful, furthermore, must be taught that Jesus Christ is Lord and Savior and that therefore the worship of

---

[9] See *GIRM* no. 269 [*DOL* 208, no. 1659].

[10] See *SCDW*, Instr. *Memoriale Domini*, May 29, 1969, [*DOL* 260, no. 2060].

latria or adoration belonging to God is owed to Christ present in this sacrament.[11]

In either case, communion must be given by the authorized minister, who shows the particle of consecrated bread to the communicants and gives it to them, saying: **The body of Christ,** to which the communicants reply: **Amen.**

In the case of communion under the appearance of wine, the liturgical regulations are to be followed exactly.[12]

10 Fragments remaining after communion are to be gathered and placed in a ciborium or in a vessel with water.

Likewise, if communion is given under the appearance of wine, the chalice or other vessel is to be washed with water.

The water used for cleansing the vessels may be drunk or poured out in a suitable place.

VI. DISPOSITIONS FOR COMMUNION

11 The eucharist, which continuously makes the paschal mystery of Christ to be present among us, is the source of every grace and of the forgiveness of sins. Nevertheless, those who intend to receive the body of the Lord must approach it with a pure conscience and proper dispositions of soul if they are to receive the effects of the paschal sacrament.

On this account the Church prescribes "that those conscious of mortal sin, even though they think themselves to be contrite, must not go to the holy eucharist without sacramental confession beforehand."[13] When there is a serious reason and no opportunity for confession, they are to make an

---

[11] See *SCDS*, Instr. *Immensae caritatis* no. [*DOL* 264, no. 2088].

[12] See General Instruction of the Roman Missal, no. 242. Congregation for Divine Worship, Instruction *Sacramentali Communione*, June 29, 1970, no. 6: *AAS* 62 (1970) 665–666.

[13] See Council of Trent, sess. 13, *Decr. de Eucharistia 7: Denz-Schön* 1646–1647; sess. 14, *Canones de sacramento Paenitentiae 9:* Denz-Schön 1709. *SCDF, Pastoral Norms on Giving General Sacramental Absolution,* June 16, 1972, Preface and Norm VI [*DOL* 361, nos. 3038 and 3044].

act of perfect contrition with the intention of confessing individually, as soon as possible, the mortal sins that they cannot confess at present.

It is desirable that those who receive communion daily or very often go to the sacrament of penance at regular intervals, depending on their circumstances.

The faithful also should look upon the eucharist as a remedy that frees them from their daily faults and preserves them from mortal sins; they should also receive an explanation of how to make use of the penitential parts of the liturgy, especially at Mass.[14]

12   Communicants are not to receive the sacrament unless they have fasted for at least one hour from food and beverages, with the exception only of water and medicine.

The elderly and those suffering from any kind of infirmity, as well as those who take care of such persons, may receive the eucharist even if they have taken something within the hour before communion.[15]

13   The union with Christ, to which the sacrament is directed, should be extended to the whole of Christian life. Thus the faithful, constantly reflecting upon the gift they have received, should carry on their daily work with thanksgiving, under the guidance of the Holy Spirit, and should bring forth fruits of rich charity.

In order to continue more surely in the thanksgiving that in the Mass is offered to God in an eminent way, those who have been nourished by communion should be encouraged to remain for some time in prayer.[16]

---

[14] See *SCR*, Instr. EuchMyst no. 35 [*DOL* 179, no. 1264].

[15] See CIC, can. 919, §§1 and 3.

[16] See *SCR*, Instr. EuchMyst no. 38 [*DOL* 179, no. 1267].

HOLY COMMUNION
OUTSIDE MASS

A. RITE OF COMMUNION WITH
THE CELEBRATION OF THE WORD

14   This rite is to be used chiefly when Mass is not celebrated or when communion is not distributed at scheduled
times. The purpose is that the people should be nourished
by the word of God. By hearing it they learn that the marvels
it proclaims reach their climax in the paschal mystery of which
the Mass is a sacramental memorial and in which they share
by communion. Nourished by God's word, they are led on
to grateful and fruitful participation in the saving mysteries.

INTRODUCTORY RITES

15   After the people have assembled and preparations for the service (see nos. 7–8) are complete, all stand for the greeting of the minister.

Greeting

The minister greets those present with these or similar words:

Brothers and sisters,
the Lord invites us (you) to his table
to share in the body of Christ:
bless him for his goodness.

The people answer: **Blessed be God for ever.**

Penitential Rite

16   The penitential rite follows, and the minister invites the people to recall their sins and to repent of them in these words:

A **My brothers and sisters,**
to prepare ourselves for this celebration,
let us call to mind our sins.

A pause for silent reflection follows.

All say:

I confess to almighty God,
and to you, my brothers and sisters,
that I have sinned through my own fault

They strike their breast:

in my thoughts and in my words,
in what I have done,
and in what I have failed to do;

and I ask blessed Mary, ever virgin,
all the angels and saints,
and you, my brothers and sisters,
to pray for me to the Lord our God.

The minister concludes:

**May almighty God have mercy on us,
forgive us our sins,
and bring us to everlasting life.**

The people answer: **Amen.**

B **My brothers and sisters,
to prepare ourselves for this celebration,
let us call to mind our sins.**

A pause for silent reflection follows.

The minister says:

Lord, we have sinned against you.

The people answer: **Lord, have mercy.**

Minister:

Lord, show us your mercy and love.

The people answer:

And grant us your salvation.

The minister concludes:

**May almighty God have mercy on us,
forgive us our sins,
and bring us to everlasting life.**

The people answer: **Amen.**

C **My brothers and sisters,**
to prepare ourselves for this celebration,
let us call to mind our sins.

> A pause for silent reflection follows.
>
> The minister, or someone else, makes the following or other invocations:
>
> Minister:

You brought us to salvation by your paschal mystery:
Lord, have mercy.

> The people answer: **Lord, have mercy.**
>
> Minister:

You renew us by the wonders of your passion:
Christ, have mercy.

> The people answer: **Christ, have mercy.**
>
> Minister:

You give us your body to make us one with your
  Easter sacrifice: Lord, have mercy.

> The people answer: **Lord, have mercy.**
>
> The minister concludes:

May almighty God have mercy on us,
forgive us our sins,
and bring us to everlasting life.

> The people answer: **Amen.**

CELEBRATION OF THE WORD OF GOD

> 17   The Liturgy of the Word now takes place as at Mass.
> Texts are chosen for the occasion either from the Mass of
> the day or from the votive Masses of the Holy Eucharist or

the Precious Blood, the readings from which are in the Lectionary. The Lectionary offers a wide range of readings which may be drawn upon for particular needs, such as the votive Mass of the Sacred Heart.

Readings

There may be one or more readings, the first being followed by a psalm or some other chant or by a period of silent prayer.

General Intercessions

The celebration of the word ends with the general intercessions.

HOLY COMMUNION

Lord's Prayer

18   After the prayer the minister goes to the place where the sacrament is reserved, takes the ciborium or pyx containing the body of the Lord, places it on the altar and genuflects. The minister then introduces the Lord's Prayer in these or similar words:

Let us pray with confidence to the Father in the words
our Savior gave us:

The minister continues with the people:

Our Father. . . .

Sign of Peace

19   The minister may invite the people in these or similar words:

Let us offer each other the sign of peace.

All make an appropriate sign of peace, according to local custom.

Invitation to Communion

20   The minister genuflects. Taking the host, the minister raises it slighty over the vessel or pyx and, facing the people, says:

**This is the Lamb of God
who takes away the sins of the world.
Happy are those who are called to his supper.**

The communicants say once:

**Lord, I am not worthy to receive you,
but only say the word and I shall be healed.**

Communion

21   If the minister receives communion, he or she says quietly:

May the body of Christ bring me to everlasting life.

The minister reverently consumes the body of Christ.

22   Then the minister takes the vessel or pyx and goes to the communicants. He or she takes a host for each one, raises it slightly, and says:

The body of Christ.

The communicant answers: **Amen,**
and receives communion.

Communion Song

23   During the distribution of communion, a hymn may be sung.

24   After communion the minister puts any particle left on the plate into the pyx, and the minister may wash his/her hands. The minister returns any remaining hosts to the tabernacle and genuflects.

Silence, Psalm, or Song of Praise

25 A period of silence may now be observed, or a psalm or song of praise may be sung.

Concluding Prayer

26 The minister then says one of the following concluding prayers:

Let us pray.

A **Lord Jesus Christ,**
you gave us the eucharist
as the memorial of your suffering and death.
May our worship of this sacrament of your body and blood
help us to experience the salvation you won for us
and the peace of the kingdom
where you live with the Father and the Holy Spirit,
one God, for ever and ever.

The people answer: **Amen.**

B **Father,**
you have brought to fulfillment the work of our redemption
through the Easter mystery of Christ your Son.
May we who faithfully proclaim his death and resurrection in these sacramental signs
experience the constant growth of your salvation in our lives.

We ask this through Christ our Lord.

C **Lord,**
you have nourished us with one bread from heaven.
Fill us with your Spirit,
and make us one in peace and love.

We ask this through Christ our Lord.

D **Lord,**
may our sharing at this holy table make us holy.
By the body and blood of Christ
join all your people in brotherly love.

We ask this through Christ our Lord.

E **Father,**
you give us food from heaven.
By our sharing in this mystery
teach us to judge wisely the things of earth
and to love the things of heaven.

Grant this through Christ our Lord.

F **Lord,**
we give thanks for these holy mysteries
which bring to us here on earth
a share in the life to come,
through Christ our Lord.

G **All-powerful God,**
you renew us with your sacraments.
Help us to thank you by lives of faithful service.

We ask this through Christ our Lord.

H **God our Father,**
you give us a share in the one bread and the one cup
and make us one in Christ.
Help us to bring your salvation and joy
to all the world.

We ask this through Christ our Lord.

I **Lord,**
   you renew us at your table with the bread of life.
   May this food strengthen us in love
   and help us to serve you in each other.

   We ask this in the name of Jesus the Lord.

J **Lord,**
   we thank you for the nourishment you give us
   through your holy gift.
   Pour out your Spirit upon us
   and in the strength of this food from heaven
   keep us single-minded in your service.

   We ask this in the name of Jesus the Lord.

K **Lord,**
   we are renewed by the breaking of one bread.
   Keep us in your love
   and help us to live the new life Christ won for us.

   Grant this in the name of Jesus the Lord.

During the Easter season the following prayers are preferred:

L **Lord,**
   you have nourished us with your Easter sacraments.
   Fill us with your Spirit
   and make us one in peace and love.

   We ask this through Christ our Lord.

M **Lord,**
   may this sharing in the sacrament of your Son
   free us from our old life of sin
   and make us your new creation.

   We ask this in the name of Jesus the Lord.

N **Almighty and ever-living Lord,**
you restored us to life
by raising Christ from death.
Strengthen us by this Easter sacrament;
may we feel its saving power in our daily life.

We ask this through Christ our Lord.

Concluding Rite

Blessing

27   The minister invokes God's blessing and, crossing himself or herself, says:

May the Lord bless us,
protect us from all evil
and bring us to everlasting life.

or:

May the almighty and merciful God bless and pro-
tect us,
the Father, and the Son, and the Holy Spirit.

The people answer: **Amen.**

Dismissal

28   Finally the minister says:

Go in the peace of Christ.

The people answer: **Thanks be to God.**

Then after the customary reverence, the minister leaves.

OUTLINE OF THE RITE

B. RITE OF COMMUNION WITH THE SHORT FORM OF THE READING OF THE WORD

29   This form of service is used when the longer, more elaborate form is unsuitable, especially when there are only one or two for communion and a true community celebration is impossible.

INTRODUCTORY RITES

30   When everything is ready (see nos. 7–8 , the minister greets the communicants.

Greeting

The minister greets those present with these or similar words:

Brothers and sisters,
the Lord invites us (you) to his table
to share in the body of Christ:
bless him for his goodness.

The people answer: **Blessed be God for ever.**

Penitential Rite

The penitential rite follows, and the minister invites the people to recall their sins and to repent of them in these words:

My brothers and sisters,
to prepare ourselves for this celebration,
let us call to mind our sins.

A pause for silent reflection follows.

All say:

I confess to almighty God,
and to you, my brothers and sisters,
that I have sinned through my own fault

They strike their breast:

in my thoughts and in my words,
in what I have done,
and in what I have failed to do;
and I ask blessed Mary, ever virgin,
all the angels and saints,
and you, my brothers and sisters,
to pray for me to the Lord our God.

The minister concludes:

May almighty God have mercy on us,
forgive us our sins,
and bring us to everlasting life.

The people answer: **Amen.**

Other forms of the penitential rite, no. 16, may be chosen.

THE SHORT FORM OF THE READING OF THE WORD

31   Omitting the celebration of the word of God, the minister or other person should read a short scriptural text referring to the bread of life.

A   John 6:54-55

Those who eat my flesh and drink my blood
  have eternal life,
  and I will raise them on the last day.
For my flesh is true food,
  and my blood is true drink.

B   John 6:54-58

Those who eat my flesh and drink my blood
  have eternal life,
  and I will raise them on the last day.
For my flesh is true food,
  and my blood is true drink.
Those who eat my flesh and drink my blood
  remain in me and I in them.
Just as the living Father sent me
  and I have life because of the Father,
  so also the one who feeds on me will have life
    because of me.
This is the bread that came down from heaven.
Unlike your ancestors who ate and still died,
  whoever eats this bread will live forever.

C   John 14:6

Jesus said to him, "I am the way and the truth and
  the life.
No one comes to the Father but through me."

D   John 14:23

Jesus said to his disciple, Jude:
   "Those who love me will keep my word,
   and my Father will love them,
   and we will come to them and make our dwelling
      with them."

E   John 15:4

Remain in me, as I remain in you.
Just as a branch cannot bear fruit on its own
   unless it remains on the vine,
   so neither can you unless you remain in me.

F   1 Corinthians 11:26

For as often as you eat this bread and drink the cup,
   you proclaim the death of the Lord until he comes.

G   1 John 4:16

We have come to know and to believe in the love
      God has for us.
God is love, and whoever remains in love
remains in God and God in him.

See nos. 133ff. of the complete ritual for a further selection
of texts.

Holy Communion

Lord's Prayer

32   The minister takes the ciborium or pyx containing the
body of the Lord, places it on the altar, and genuflects. The
minister then introduces the Lord's Prayer in these or similar
words:

Let us pray with confidence to the Father
in the words our Savior gave us:

The minister continues with the people:

Our Father. . . .

Invitation to Communion

33 The minister genuflects. Taking the host, the minister raises it slightly over the vessel or pyx and, facing the people, says:

This is the Lamb of God
who takes away the sins of the world.
Happy are those who are called to his supper.

The communicants say once:

Lord, I am not worthy to receive you,
but only say the word and I shall be healed.

Communion

34 If the minister receives communion, he or she says quietly:

May the body of Christ bring me to everlasting life.

The minister reverently consumes the body of Christ.

35 Then the minister takes the vessel or pyx and goes to the communicants. He or she takes a host for each one, raises it slightly, and says:

The body of Christ.

The communicant answers:

Amen, and receives communion.

36 After communion the minister puts any particles left on the plate into the pyx, and the minister may wash his/her hands. The minister returns any remaining hosts to the tabernacle and genuflects.

Silence, Psalm, or Song of Praise

A period of silence may now be observed, or a psalm or song of praise may be sung.

Concluding Prayer

37   The minister then says the concluding prayer:

Let us pray.

A **Lord Jesus Christ,**
   you gave us the eucharist as the memorial of your suffering and death.
   May our worship of this sacrament of your body and blood
   help us to experience the salvation you won for us and the peace of the kingdom
   where you live with the Father and the Holy Spirit, one God, for ever and ever.

The people answer: **Amen.**

Other prayers may be chosen:

B **Father,**
   you have brought to fulfillment the work of our redemption
   through the Easter mystery of Christ your Son.
   May we who faithfully proclaim his death and resurrection in these sacramental signs
   experience the constant growth of your salvation in our lives.

   We ask this through Christ our Lord.

C **Lord,**
   you have nourished us with one bread from heaven.

Fill us with your Spirit,
and make us one in peace and love.

We ask this through Christ our Lord.

D Lord,
may our sharing at this holy table make us holy.
By the body and blood of Christ
join all your people in brotherly love.

We ask this through Christ our Lord.

E Father,
you give us food from heaven.
By our sharing in this mystery
teach us to judge wisely the things of earth
and to love the things of heaven.

Grant this through Christ our Lord.

F Lord,
we give thanks for these holy mysteries
which bring to us here on earth
a share in the life to come,
through Christ our Lord.

G All-powerful God,
you renew us with your sacraments.
Help us to thank you by lives of faithful service.

We ask this through Christ our Lord.

H God our Father,
you give us a share in the one bread and the one cup
and make us one in Christ.
Help us to bring your salvation and joy to all the
world.

We ask this through Christ our Lord.

I **Lord,**
you renew us at your table with the bread of life
May this food strengthen us in love
and help us to serve you in each other.

We ask this in the name of Jesus the Lord.

J **Lord,**
we thank you for the nourishment you give us
through your holy gift.

Pour out your Spirit upon us
and in the strength of this food from heaven
keep us single-minded in your service.

We ask this in the name of Jesus the Lord.

K **Lord,**
we are renewed by the breaking of one bread.
Keep us in your love
and help us to live the new life Christ won for us.

Grant this in the name of Jesus the Lord.

During the Easter season the following prayers are preferred:

L **Lord,**
you have nourished us with your Easter sacraments.
Fill us with your Spirit
and make us one in peace and love.

We ask this through Christ our Lord.

M **Lord,**
may this sharing in the sacrament of your Son
free us from our old life of sin
and make us your new creation.

We ask this in the name of Jesus the Lord.

N **Almighty and ever-living Lord,**
you restored us to life
by raising Christ from death.
Strengthen us by this Easter sacrament;
may we feel its saving power in our daily life.

We ask this through Christ our Lord.

CONCLUDING RITE

Blessing

38   The minister invokes God's blessing, and crossing
himself or herself says:

May the Lord bless us,
protect us from all evil
and bring us to everlasting life.

or:

May the almighty and merciful God bless and pro-
tect us,
the Father, and the Son, and the Holy Spirit.

The people answer: **Amen.**

Dismissal

39   Finally the minister says:

Go in the peace of Christ.

The people answer: **Thanks be to God.**

Then after the customary reverence, the minister leaves.

CHAPTER 2

ADMINISTRATION OF COMMUNION AND VIATICUM TO THE SICK BY AN EXTRAORDINARY MINISTER

INTRODUCTION

40   A priest or deacon administers communion or viaticum to the sick in the manner prescribed by the *Rite of Anointing and Pastoral Care of the Sick.* When an acolyte or an extraordinary minister, duly appointed, gives communion to the sick, the rite here described is followed.

41   Those who cannot receive communion in the form of bread may receive it in the form of wine. The precious blood must be carried to the sick person in a vessel so secured as to eliminate all danger of spilling. The sacrament should be administered with due regard to the individual concerned, and the rite for giving communion under both kinds provides a choice of methods. If all the precious blood is not consumed, the minister himself must consume it and then wash the vessel as required.

OUTLINE OF THE RITE

A. THE ORDINARY RITE OF COMMUNION OF THE SICK
   Introductory Rite
   The Short Form of the Reading of the Word
   Holy Communion
   Concluding Rite

A. THE ORDINARY RITE OF COMMUNION OF THE SICK

INTRODUCTORY RITE

Greeting

42   The minister approaches the sick person and greets him or her and the others present in a friendly manner. The minister may use this greeting:

Peace to this house and to all who live it.

Any other customary form of greeting from scripture may be used. Then he places the sacrament on the table, and all adore it.

Penitential Rite

43   The minister invites the sick person and those present to recall their sins and to repent of them in these words:

A **My brothers and sisters,**
to prepare ourselves for this celebration,
let us call to mind our sins.

A pause for silent reflection follows.

All say:

I confess to almighty God,
and to you, my brothers and sisters,
that I have sinned through my own fault

They strike their breast:

in my thoughts and in my words,
in what I have done,
and in what I have failed to do;

and I ask blessed Mary, ever virgin,
all the angels and saints,
and you, my brothers and sisters,
to pray for me to the Lord our God.

The minister concludes:

May almighty God have mercy on us,
forgive us our sins,
and bring us to everlasting life.

The people answer: **Amen.**

B My brothers and sisters,
to prepare ourselves for this celebration,
let us call to mind our sins.

A pause for silent reflection follows.

The minister says:

Lord, we have sinned against you.

The people answer: **Lord, have mercy.**

Minister:

Lord, show us your mercy and love.

The people answer: **And grant us your salvation.**

The minister concludes:

May almighty God have mercy on us,
forgive us our sins,
and bring us to everlasting life.

The people answer: **Amen.**

C My brothers and sisters,
to prepare ourselves for this celebration,
let us call to mind our sins.

A pause for silent reflection follows.

The minister, or someone else, makes the following or other invocations:

Minister:

You brought us to salvation by your paschal mystery: Lord, have mercy.

The people answer: **Lord, have mercy.**

Minister:

You renew us by the wonders of your passion: Christ, have mercy.

The people answer: **Christ, have mercy.**

Minister:

You give us your body to make us one with your Easter sacrifice: Lord, have mercy.

The people answer: **Lord have mercy.**

The minister concludes:

**May almighty God have mercy on us,
forgive us our sins,
and bring us to everlasting life.**

The people answer: **Amen.**

THE SHORT FORM OF THE READING OF THE WORD

44   A brief passage from sacred scripture may then be read by
one of those present or by the minister.

A   John 6:54-58

Those who eat my flesh and drink my blood
  have eternal life,
   and I will raise them on the last day.
For my flesh is true food,
  and my blood is true drink.
Those who eat my flesh and drink my blood
  remain in me and I in them.
Just as the living Father sent me
  and I have life because of the Father,
   so also the one who feeds on me will have life
    because of me.
This is the bread that came down from heaven.
Unlike your ancestors who ate and still died,
  whoever eats this bread will life forever.

B   John 14:6

Jesus said to him:
"I am the way, and the truth, and the life.
No one comes to the Father except through me."

C   John 14:23

Jesus answered and said to him,
"Those who love me will keep my word,
and my Father will love them,
and we will come to them and make our dwelling
  with them."

D   John 15:4

Remain in me, as I remain in you.
Just as a branch cannot bear fruit on its own

unless it remains on the vine,
so neither can you unless you remain in me.

E   1 Corinthians 11:26

Every time, then, you eat this bread and drink this
cup,
You proclaim the death of the Lord until he comes.

F   1 John 4:16

We have come to know and to believe in the love
   God has for us.
God is love, and whoever, remains in love
remains in God and God in him.

HOLY COMMUNION

Lord's Prayer

45   The minister then introduces the Lord's Prayer in
these or similar words:

Now let us pray together to the Father in the words
given us by our Lord Jesus Christ.

The minister continues with the people:

Our Father. . . .

Invitation to Communion

46   Then the minister shows the holy eucharist, saying:

This is the Lamb of God
who takes away the sins of the world.
Happy are those who are called to his supper.

The sick person and the other communicants say once:

Lord, I am not worthy to receive you,
but only say the word and I shall be healed.

Communion

47 The minister goes to the sick person and, showing him or her the sacrament, says:

The body of Christ (or: **The blood of Christ**).

The sick person answers:

Amen, and receives communion.

Others present then receive in the usual manner.

Concluding Prayer

48 After communion the minister washes the vessel as usual. A period of silence may now be observed.

The minister then says one of the following concluding prayers:

Let us pray.

A **God our Father, almighty and eternal,**
we confidently call upon you,
that the body [and blood] of Christ
which our brother (sister) has received
may bring him (her)
lasting health in mind and body.

We ask this through Christ our Lord.

The people answer: **Amen.**

B **Father,**
you have brought to fulfillment the work of our
redemption
through the Easter mystery of Christ your Son.
May we who faithfully proclaim his death and resur-
rection in these sacramental signs

experience the constant growth of your salvation in
   our lives.

We ask this through Christ our Lord.

C Lord,
you have nourished us with one bread from heaven.
Fill us with your Spirit,
and make us one in peace and love.

We ask this through Christ our Lord.

D Lord,
may our sharing at this holy table make us holy.
By the body and blood of Christ
join all your people in brotherly love.

We ask this through Christ our Lord.

E Father,
you give us food from heaven.
By our sharing in this mystery
teach us to judge wisely the things of earth
and to love the things of heaven.

Grant this through Christ our Lord.

F Lord,
we give thanks for these holy mysteries
which bring to us here on earth
a share in the life to come,
through Christ our Lord.

G All-powerful God,
you renew us with your sacraments.
Help us to thank you by lives of faithful service.

We ask this through Christ our Lord.

H God our Father,
you give us a share in the one bread and the one cup
and make us one in Christ.
Help us to bring your salvation and joy
to all the world.

We ask this through Christ our Lord.

I Lord,
you renew us at your table with the bread of life.
May this food strengthen us in love
and help us to serve you in each other.

We ask this in the name of Jesus the Lord.

J Lord,
we thank you for the nourishment you give us
through your holy gift.
Pour out your Spirit upon us
and in the strength of this food from heaven
keep us single-minded in your service.

We ask this in the name of Jesus the Lord.

K Lord,
we are renewed by the breaking of one bread.
Keep us in your love
and help us to live the new life Christ won for us.

Grant this in the name of Jesus the Lord.

During the Easter season the following prayers are preferred:

L Lord,
you have nourished us with your Easter sacraments.
Fill us with your Spirit
and make us one in peace and love.

We ask this through Christ our Lord.

M **Lord,**
may this sharing in the sacrament of your Son
free us from our old life of sin
and make us your new creation.

We ask this in the name of Jesus the Lord.

N **Almighty and ever-living Lord,**
you restored us to life
by raising Christ from death.
Strengthen us by this Easter sacrament;
may we feel its saving power in our daily life.

We ask this through Christ our Lord.

Concluding Rite

Blessing

49 Then the minister invokes God's blessing, and crossing him or herself says:

May the Lord bless us,
protect us from all evil
and bring us to everlasting life.

or:

May the almighty and merciful God
bless and protect us,
the Father, and the Son, and the Holy Spirit.

The people answer: **Amen.**

OUTLINE OF THE RITE

B. SHORT RITE OF COMMUNION OF THE SICK
   Antiphon
   Invitation to Communion
   Distribution of Communion
   Concluding Prayer

B. SHORT RITE OF COMMUNION OF THE SICK

50   This shorter rite is to be used when communion is given in different rooms of the same building, such as a hospital. Elements taken from the ordinary rite may be added according to circumstances.

ANTIPHON

51   The rite may begin in the church or chapel or in the first room, where the minister says one of the following antiphons:

A **How holy this feast**
   in which Christ is our food:
   his passion is recalled,
   grace fills our hearts,
   and we receive a pledge of the glory to come.

B **How gracious you are, Lord:**
   your gift of bread from heaven
   reveals a Father's love and brings us perfect joy.
   You fill the hungry with good things
   and send away empty the rich in their pride.

C Body of Jesus, born of the Virgin Mary,
 body bowed in agony,
 raised upon the cross
 and offered for us in sacrifice,
 body pierced and flowing with blood and water,
 come at the hour of our death
 as our living bread,
 the foretaste of eternal glory:
 come, Lord Jesus,
 loving and gracious Son of Mary.

D I am the living bread
 come down from heaven.
 If anyone eats this bread
 he shall live for ever.
 The bread I will give is my flesh
 for the life of the world.

INVITATION TO COMMUNION

52 Then the minister may be escorted by someone carrying a candle. The minister says to all the sick persons in the same room or to each communicant individually:

This is the Lamb of God
who takes away the sins of the world.
Happy are those who are called to his supper.

The one who is to receive communion then says once:

Lord, I am not worthy to receive you,
but only say the word and I shall be healed.

COMMUNION

He or she receives communion in the usual manner.

CONCLUDING PRAYER

53   The rite is concluded with a prayer (see no. 48) which
may be said in the church or chapel or in the last room:

Let us pray.

**God our Father, almighty and eternal,
we confidently call upon you,
that the body [and blood] of Christ
which our brother (sister) has received
may bring him (her)
lasting health in mind and body.**

We ask this through Christ our Lord.

The people answer: **Amen.**

Other prayers, no. 48, may be chosen.

C. VIATICUM

54   When in their passage from this life Christians are strengthened by the body and blood of Christ in viaticum, they have the pledge of the resurrection that the Lord promised ''Those who eat my flesh and drink my blood have eternal life, and I will raise them up on the last day'' (John 6:54).

When possible, viaticum should be received within Mass so that the sick person may receive communion under both kinds. Communion received as viaticum should be considered a special sign of participation in the mystery which is celebrated in the eucharist: the mystery of the death of the Lord and his passage to the Father.[1]

55   All baptized Christians who are able to receive communion are bound to receive viaticum by reason of the precept to receive communion when in danger of death from any cause. Priests with pastoral responsibility must see that the celebration of this sacrament is not delayed, but that the faithful are nourished by it while still in full possession of their faculties.[2]

56   It is also desirable that during the celebration of viaticum, Christians renew the faith professed at their baptism, by which they became adopted children of God and coheirs of the promise of eternal life.

57   The ordinary ministers of viaticum are the pastor and his assistants, chaplains, and, for all staying in the house, the superior in clerical religious institutes or societies of apostolic life.

In case of necessity or with at least the presumed permission of the competent minister, any priest or deacon is to give viaticum, or, if no ordained minister is available, any member of the faithful who has been duly appointed.

---

[1] See Congregation of Rites, Instruction *Eucharisticum mysterium*, May 25, 1967, nos. 36, 39, 41 [DOL 179, nos. 1265, 1268, 1270].

[2] See Congregation of Rites, Instruction *Eucharisticum Mysterium*, May 25, 1967, no. 39 [DOL 179, no. 1268].

OUTLINE OF THE RITE

C. VIATICUM
Introductory Rite
The Short Form of Reading of the Word
Profession of Baptismal Faith
Prayer for the Sick Person
Viaticum
Concluding Rite

INTRODUCTORY RITE

Greeting

58   The minister approaches the sick person and greets him or her and the others present in a friendly manner. The minister may use this greeting:

Peace to this house and to all who live in it.

Any other customary form of greeting from scripture may be used. Then the minister places the sacrament on the table, and all adore it.

Instruction

59   Afterward the minister addresses those present, using the following instruction or one better suited to the sick person's condition:

My brothers and sisters:

Before our Lord Jesus Christ passed from this world to return to his Father, he gave us the sacrament of his body and blood. This is the promise of our resurrection, the food and drink for our journey as we pass from this life to join him. United in the love of Christ, let us ask God to give strength to our brother (sister).

A period of silent prayer then follows.

Penitential Rite

60   The minister invites the sick person and all present to recall their sins and to repent of them in these words:

My brothers and sisters,
to prepare ourselves for this celebration,
let us call to mind our sins.

A pause for silent reflection follows.

All say:

I confess to almighty God,
and to you, my brothers and sisters,
that I have sinned through my own fault

They strike their breast:

in my thoughts and in my words,
in what I have done,
and in what I have failed to do;
and I ask blessed Mary, ever virgin,
all the angels and saints,
and you, my brothers and sisters,
to pray for me to the Lord our God.

The minister concludes:

May almighty God have mercy on us,
forgive us our sins,
and bring us to everlasting life.

The people answer: **Amen.**

Other forms of the penitential rite, no. 43, may be chosen.

The Short Form of the Reading of the Word

61 It is most fitting that one of those present or the minister read a brief text from scripture: (see no. **44**).

John 6:54-58
John 14:6
John 14:23
John 15:4
1 Corinthians 11:26
1 John 4:16

Profession of Baptismal Faith

62 It is desirable that the sick person renew his or her baptismal profession of faith before he or she receives viaticum. The minister gives a brief instruction and then asks the following questions:

Do you believe in God, the Father almighty, creator of heaven and earth?

℟. **I do.**

Do you believe in Jesus Christ, his only Son, our Lord, who was born of the Virgin Mary, was crucified, died, and was buried, rose from the dead, and is now seated at the right hand of the Father?

℟. **I do.**

Do you believe in the Holy Spirit, the holy Catholic Church, the communion of saints, the forgiveness of sins, the resurrection of the body, and life everlasting?

℟. **I do.**

Prayer for the Sick Person

63   If the condition of the sick person permits, a brief
litany is recited in these or similar words. The sick person,
if he or she is able, and all present respond:

**My brothers and sisters, let us pray with one mind
and heart to our Lord Jesus Christ:**

**Lord, you loved us to the end, and you accepted
death that we might have life: hear our prayer for
our brother (sister).**

℟. **Lord, hear our prayer.**

**Lord, you said: ''He who eats my flesh and drinks
my blood has eternal life'': hear our prayer for our
brother (sister).**

℟. **Lord, hear our prayer.**

**Lord, you invite us to the banquet of your kingdom,
where there will be no more pain or mourning, no
more sorrow or separation: hear our prayer for our
brother (sister).**

℟. **Lord, hear our prayer.**

Viaticum

Lord's Prayer

64   The minister introduces the Lord's Prayer in these
or similar words:

**Now let us pray together to the Father in the words
given us by our Lord Jesus Christ.**

All continue:

Our Father. . . .

Invitation to Communion

65   Then the minister shows the holy eucharist to those present, saying:

This is the Lamb of God
who takes away the sins of the world.
Happy are those who are called to his supper.

The sick person and all who are to receive communion say once:

Lord, I am not worthy to receive you,
but only say the word and I shall be healed.

Communion

66   The minister goes to the sick person and, showing him or her the sacrament, says:

The body of Christ (or: **The blood of Christ**).

The sick person answers: **Amen.**

Immediately, or after giving communion, the minister adds:

May the Lord Jesus Christ protect you and lead you
to eternal life.

The sick person answers: **Amen.**

Others present then receive communion in the usual manner.

67   After communion the minister washes the vessel as usual. Then a period of silence may be observed.

CONCLUDING RITE

Concluding Prayer

68   The minister says the concluding prayer:

Let us pray.

A **Father,**
  your son, Jesus Christ, is our way, our truth, and
    our life.
  Our brother (sister) N. entrusts himself (herself) to
    you
  with full confidence in all your promises.
  Refresh him (her) with the body and blood of your
    Son
  and lead him (her) to your kingdom in peace.
  We ask this through Christ our Lord.

  ℟ **Amen.**

B **Lord,**
  you are the source of eternal health
  for those who believe in you.
  May our brother (sister) N.,
  who has been refreshed
  with food and drink from heaven,
  safely reach your kingdom of light and life.

  We ask this through Christ our Lord.

  ℟ **Amen.**

The minister makes the sign of the cross on himself or herself while saying:

May the almighty and merciful God bless and protect us the Father, and the Son and the Holy Spirit.

℟ **Amen.**

The minister and others present may then give the sick person the sign of peace.

PART II
PASTORAL CARE
OF THE SICK

Chapter 3

VISITS TO THE SICK

INTRODUCTION

I was sick, and you visited me.

69   The prayers contained in this chapter follow the common pattern of reading, response, prayer, and blessing. This pattern is provided as an example of what can be done and may be adapted as necessary. The minister may wish to invite those present to prepare for the reading from Scripture, perhaps by a brief introduction or through a moment of silence.

70   The sick should be encouraged to pray when they are alone or with their families, friends, or those who care for them. Their prayer should be drawn primarily from Scripture. The sick person and others may help to plan the celebration, for example, by choosing the prayers and readings. Those making these choices should keep in mind the condition of the sick person.

   The passages found in this chapter and those included in Part IV speak of the mystery of human suffering in the words, works, and life of Christ. Occasionally, for example, on the Lord's Day, the sick may feel more involved in the worship of the community from which they are separated if the readings used are those assigned for that day in the lectionary. Prayers may also be drawn from the psalms or from other prayers or litanies. The sick should be helped in making this form of prayer, and the minister should always be ready to pray with them.

71   The minister should encourage the sick person to offer his or her sufferings in union with Christ and to join in prayer for the Church and the world. Some examples of particular

intentions which may be suggested to the sick person are: for
peace in the world; for a deepening of the life of the Spirit
in the local Church; for the pope and the bishops; for people
suffering in a particular disaster.

OUTLINE OF THE RITE

INTRODUCTION
  Reading
  Response
  The Lord's Prayer
  Concluding Prayer
  Blessing

READING

72   The word of God is proclaimed by one of those present or by the minister. An appropriate reading from Part
IV or one of the following readings may be used:

A **A reading from Acts of the Apostles**   3:1-10

*In the name of Jesus and the power of his Church, there is
salvation—even liberation from sickness.*

**Peter and John were going up to the temple area
  for the three o'clock hour of prayer.
And a man lame from birth
  was carried and placed
  at the gate of the temple called ''the Beautiful
    Gate''**

every day to beg for alms from the people who
entered the temple.

When he saw Peter and John about to go into the
temple,

he asked for alms.

But Peter looked intently at the man, as did John,
and said, "Look at us."

The man paid attention to them, expecting to receive
something from them.

Peter said, "I have neither silver nor gold, but what
I do have I give you:

in the name of Jesus Christ the Nazorean, rise
and walk."

Then Peter took him by the right hand and raised
him up,

and immediately the man's feet and ankles grew
strong.

The man leaped up, stood, and walked around,
and went into the temple with them,

walking and jumping and praising God.

When all the people saw him walking and praising
God,

they recognized him as the one

who used to sit begging at the Beautiful Gate of
the temple,

and they were filled with amazement and aston-
ishment

at what had happened to him.

The word of the Lord.

B **A reading from the holy gospel according to Matthew** 8:14-17

Jesus fulfills the prophetic figure of the servant of God taking upon himself and relieving the sufferings of God's people.

Jesus entered the house of Peter,
   and saw Peter's mother-in-law lying in bed with
      a fever.
Jesus touched her hand, the fever left her,
   and she rose and waited on him.

When it was evening, people brought Jesus many
   who were possessed by demons,
      and he drove out the spirits by a word and cured
         all the sick,
      to fulfill what had been said by Isaiah the prophet:
         "He took away our infirmities
            and bore our diseases."

                                    The gospel of the Lord.

RESPONSE

73   A brief period of silence may be observed after the reading of the word of God. An appropriate psalm from Part IV or one of the following psalms may be used:

A   Psalm 102

   ℟. (2) **O Lord, hear my prayer and let my cry
      come to you.**

LORD, hear my prayer;
let my cry come to you.
Do not hide your face from me
now that I am in distress.
Turn your ear to me;
when I call, answer me quickly. ℟.

God has shattered my strength in mid-course,
has cut short my days.
I plead, O my God,
do not take me in the midst of my days.
Your years last through all generations. R⁊.

Let this be written for the next generation,
for a people not yet born,
that they may praise the LORD:
"The LORD looked down from his holy height,
viewed the earth from heaven,
To attend to the groaning of the prisoners,
to release those doomed to die." R⁊.

B   Psalm 27

R⁊. (1) The Lord is my light and my salvation.

The LORD is my light and my salvation;
whom do I fear?
The LORD is my life's refuge;
of whom am I afraid? R⁊.

One thing I ask of the LORD;
this I seek:
To dwell in the LORD's house
all the days of my life,
To gaze on the LORD's beauty,
to visit his temple. R⁊.

For God will hide me in his shelter
in time of trouble,
will conceal me in the cover of his tent;
and set me high upon a rock. R⁊.

The minister may then give a brief explanation of the reading, applying it to the needs of the sick person and those
who are looking after him or her.

The Lord's Prayer

74 The minister introduces the Lord's Prayer in these or similar words:

Now let us offer together the prayer our Lord Jesus Christ taught us:

All say:

Our Father. . . .

Concluding Prayer

75 The minister says a concluding prayer. One of the following may be used:

A **Father,**
your Son accepted our sufferings
to teach us the virtue of patience in human illness.
Hear the prayers we offer for our sick brother/sister.
May all who suffer pain, illness, or disease
realize that they have been chosen to be saints
and know that they are joined to Christ
in his suffering for the salvation of the world.

We ask this through Christ our Lord.

℟. **Amen.**

B **All-powerful and ever-living God,**
the lasting health of all who believe in you,
hear us as we ask your loving help for the sick;
restore their health,
that they may again offer joyful thanks in your Church.

Grant this through Christ our Lord.

℟. **Amen.**

C **All-powerful and ever-living God,**
we find security in your forgiveness.
Give us serenity and peace of mind;
may we rejoice in your gifts of kindness
and use them always for your glory and our good.

We ask this in the name of Jesus the Lord.

R̷. **Amen.**

BLESSING

76 The minister may give a blessing. One of the following may be used:

A **All praise and glory is yours, Lord our God,**
for you have called us to serve you in love.
Bless N.
so that he/she may bear this illness
in union with your Son's obedient suffering.
Restore him/her to health,
and lead him/her to glory.

We ask this through Christ our Lord.

R̷. **Amen.**

B For an elderly person
All praise and glory are yours, Lord our God,
for you have called us to serve you in love.
Bless all who have grown old in your service
and give N. strength and courage
to continue to follow Jesus your Son.

We ask this through Christ our Lord.

R̷. **Amen.**

The minister invokes God's blessing and makes the sign of the cross on himself or herself, while saying:

**May the Lord bless us,
protect us from all evil,
and bring us to everlasting life.**

℞. **Amen.**

The minister may then trace the sign of the cross on the sick person's forehead.

Chapter 4

VISITS TO A SICK CHILD

INTRODUCTION

Let the children come to me; do not keep them back from me.

77   The following readings, prayers, and blessings will help the minister to pray with sick children and their families. They are provided as an example of what can be done and may be adapted as necessary. The minister may wish to invite those present to prepare for the reading from Scripture, perhaps by a brief introduction or through a moment of silence.

78   If the child does not already know the minister, the latter should seek to establish a friendly and easy relationship with the child. Therefore, the greeting which begins the visit should be an informal one.

79   The minister should help sick children to understand that the sick are very special in the eyes of God because they are suffering as Christ suffered and because they can offer their sufferings for the salvation of the world.

80   In praying with the sick child the minister chooses, together with the child and the family if possible, suitable elements of common prayer in the form of a brief liturgy of the word. This may consist of a reading from Scripture, simple one-line prayers taken from Scripture which can be repeated by the child, other familiar prayers such as the Lord's Prayer, the Hail Mary, litanies, or a simple form of the general intercessions.

OUTLINE OF THE RITE

INTRODUCTION
Reading
Response
The Lord's Prayer
Concluding Prayer
Blessing

READING

81   One of the following readings may be used for a brief
liturgy of the word. Other readings may be chosen, for example: **Mark 5:21-23, 35-43,** *Jesus raises the daughter of Jairus
and gives her back to her parents:* **Mark 9:14-27,** *Jesus cures a
boy and gives him back to his father,* **Luke 7:11-15,** *Jesus raises
a young man, the only son of his mother, and gives him back to
her;* **John 4:46-53,** *Jesus gives his second sign by healing an offi-
cial's son.* In addition, other stories concerning the Lord's
healing ministry may be found suitable, especially if told
with the simplicity and clarity of one of the children's ver-
sions of Scripture.

A **A reading from the holy gospel
according to Mark**   9:33-37

*Jesus proposes the child as the ideal of those who would enter the
kingdom.*

**Jesus and his disciples came to Capernaum and, once
    inside the house,**
Jesus began to ask the disciples,
"What were you arguing about on the way?"
But they remained silent.
**For they had been discussing among themselves on
    the way**
who was the greatest.
**Then Jesus sat down, called the Twelve, and said to
    them,**

"Whoever wishes to be first,
shall be the last of all and the servant of all."
Taking a child, Jesus placed it in the midst of the
disciples,
and putting his arms around the child, he said to
them,
"Whoever receives one child such as this in my
name, receives me;
and whoever receives me,
receives not me but the One who sent me."

The gospel of the Lord.

B A reading from the holy gospel
according to Mark   10:13-16

Jesus welcomes the children and lays his hands on them.

People were bringing children to Jesus that he
might touch them,
but the disciples rebuked them.
When Jesus saw this he became indignant and
said to the disciples,
"Let the children come to me; do not pre-
vent them,
for the kingdom of God belongs to such as
these.
Amen, I say to you,
whoever does not accept the kingdom of God
like a child
will not enter it."
Then Jesus embraced the children and blessed
them,
placing his hands on them.

The gospel of the Lord.

RESPONSE

82   After the reading of the word of God, time may be set apart for silent reflection if the child is capable of this form of prayer. The minister should also explain the meaning of the reading to those present, adapting it to their circumstances.

The minister may then help the child and the family to respond to the word of God. The following short responsory may be used:

Jesus, come to me.
—Jesus, come to me.

Jesus, put your hand on me.
—Jesus, put your hand on me.

Jesus, bless me.
—Jesus, bless me.

THE LORD'S PRAYER

83   The minister introduces the Lord's Prayer in these or similar words:

Let us pray to the Father using those words which Jesus himself used:

All say:
Our Father. . . .

CONCLUDING PRAYER

84   The minister says a concluding prayer. One of the following may be used:

A **God of love,**
ever caring,
ever strong,
stand by us in our time of need.

Watch over your child N. who is sick,
look after him/her in every danger,
and grant him/her your healing and peace.

We ask this in the name of Jesus the Lord.

℞. Amen

B Father,
in your love
you gave us Jesus
to help us rise triumphant over grief and pain.
Look on your child N. who is sick
and see in his/her sufferings those of your Son.

Grant N. a share in the strength you granted your
   Son
that he/she too may be a sign
of your goodness, kindness, and loving care.

We ask this in the name of Jesus the Lord.

℞. Amen.

Blessing

85   The minister makes a sign of the cross on the child's
forehead, saying one of the following:

A N., when you were baptized,
you were marked with the cross of Jesus.
I (we) make this cross ✝ on your forehead
and ask the Lord to bless you,
and restore you to health.

℞. Amen.

B **All praise and glory is yours, heavenly God,**
for you have called us to serve you in love.
Have mercy on us and listen to our prayer
as we ask you to help N.

Bless ✛ your beloved child,
and restore him/her to health
in the name of Jesus the Lord.

℞. **Amen.**

Each one present may in turn trace the sign of the cross on
the child's forehead, in silence.

The minister invokes God's blessing and makes the sign
of the cross on himself or herself, while saying:

May the Lord bless us,
protect us from all evil,
and bring us to everlasting life.

℞. **Amen.**

Part III
PASTORAL CARE
OF THE DYING

CHAPTER 5

COMMENDATION
OF THE DYING

INTRODUCTION

Into your hands, Lord, I commend my spirit.

86   In viaticum the dying person is united with Christ in his passage out of this world to the Father. Through the prayers for the commendation of the dying contained in this chapter, the Church helps to sustain this union until it is brought to fulfillment after death.

87   Christians have the responsibility of expressing their union in Christ by joining the dying person in prayer for God's mercy and for confidence in Christ. In particular, the presence of a priest or deacon shows more clearly that the Christian dies in the communion of the Church. He should assist the dying person and those present in the recitation of the prayers of commendation and, following death, he should lead those present in the prayer after death. If the priest or deacon is unable to be present because of other serious pastoral obligations, other members of the community should be prepared to assist with these prayers and should have the texts readily available to them.

88   The minister may choose texts from among the prayers, litanies, aspirations, psalms, and readings provided in this chapter, or others may be added. In the selection of these texts the minister should keep in mind the condition and piety of both the dying person and the members of the family who are present. The prayers are best said in a slow, quite voice, alternating with periods of silence. If possible, the minister says one or more of the brief prayer formulas with the dying person. These may be softly repeated two or three times.

89   These texts are intended to help the dying person, if still conscious, to face the natural human anxiety about death by imitating Christ in his patient suffering and dying. The Christian will be helped to surmount his or her fear in the hope of heavenly life and resurrection through the power of Christ, who destroyed the power of death by his own dying.

Even if the dying person is not conscious, those who are present will draw consolation from these prayers and come to a better understanding of the paschal character of Christian death. This may be visibly expressed by making the sign of the cross on the forehead of the dying person, who was first signed with the cross at baptism.

90   Immediately after death has occurred, all may kneel while one of those present leads the prayers given on pp. 88–92.

OUTLINE OF THE RITE

INTRODUCTION
  Short Texts
  Reading
  Litany of the Saints
  Prayer of Commendation
  Prayer after Death
  Prayer for the Family and Friends

SHORT TEXTS

91   One or more of the following short texts may be recited with the dying person. If necessary, they may be softly repeated two or three times.

A   Romans 8:35

Who can separate us from the love of Christ?

B   Romans 14:8

Whether we live or die, we are the Lord's.

C   2 Corinthians 5:1

We have an everlasting home in heaven.

D   1 Thessalonians 4:17

We shall be with the Lord for ever.

E   1 John 3:2

We shall see God as he really is.

F   1 John 3:14

**We have passed from death to life
because we love each other.**

G   Psalm 25:1

To you, LORD, I lift up my soul.

H   Psalm 27:1

The LORD is my light and my salvation.

I   Psalm 27:13

**I believe that I shall see the goodness of the
LORD in the land of the living.**

J   Psalm 42:3

My soul thirsts for the living God.

K   Psalm 23:4

**Though I walk in the shadow of death,
I will fear no evil,
for you are with me.**

L   Matthew 25:34

**Come, blessed of my Father,
says the Lord Jesus,
and take possession of the kingdom
prepared for you.**

M   Luke 23:43

**The Lord Jesus says,
today you will be with me in paradise.**

N   John 14:2

**In my Father's home
there are many dwelling places,
says the Lord Jesus.**

O   John 14:2-3

**The Lord Jesus says,
I go to prepare a place for you,
and I will come again to take you to myself.**

P   John 17:24

**I desire that where I am,
they also may be with me,
says the Lord Jesus.**

Q   John 6:40

**Everyone who believes in the Son
has eternal life.**

R   Psalm 31:5a

**Into your hands, LORD,
I commend my spirit.**

S   Acts 7:59

Lord Jesus, receive my spirit.

T

Holy Mary, pray for me.

U

Saint Joseph, pray for me.

V

**Jesus, Mary, and Joseph,
assist me in my last agony.**

READING

92   The word of God is proclaimed by one of those present or by the minister. Selections from Part IV or from the
following readings may be used:

A   Job 19:23-27

*Job's act of faith is a model for our own; God is the God of the
living.*

**Job spoke, saying:
"Oh, would that my words were written down!
   Would that they were inscribed in a record:
that with an iron chisel and with lead
   they were cut in the rock forever!
But as for me, I know that my Vindicator lives,
   and that he will at last stand forth upon the dust;
whom I myself shall see."**

B   Psalm 23

The LORD is my shepherd;
there is nothing I lack.
In green pastures you let me graze;
to safe waters you lead me;
you restore my strength.
You guide me along the right path
for the sake of your name.
Even when I walk through a dark valley,
I fear no harm for you are at my side;
your rod and staff give me courage.
You set a table before me
as my enemies watch;
You anoint my head with oil;
my cup overflows.
Only goodness and love will pursue me
all the days of my life;
I will dwell in the house of the LORD
for years to come.

C   Psalm 25

I lift up my soul,
to my God.
Make known to me your ways, LORD;
teach me your paths.
Guide me in your truth and teach me,
for you are God my savior.
For you I wait all the long day,
because of your goodness, LORD.
Remember your compassion and love, O LORD
for they are ages old.
Remember no more the sins of my youth;
remember me only in light of your love.
Good and upright is the LORD,
who shows sinners the way,
Guides the humble rightly,
and teaches the humble the way.
All the paths of the LORD are faithful love
toward those who honor the covenant demands.
For the sake of your name, LORD,
pardon my guilt, though it is great.

D   Psalm 91

You who dwell in the shelter of the Most High,
who abide in the shadow of the Almighty,
Say to the LORD, "My refuge and my fortress,
my God in whom I trust."
God will rescue you from the fowler's snare,
from the destroying plague,
will shelter you with pinions,
spread wings that you may take refuge;
God's faithfulness is a protecting shield.
You shall not fear the terror of the night
nor the arrow that flies by day,
Nor the pestilence that roams in darkness,
nor the plague that ravages at noon.
Though a thousand fall at your side,
ten thousand at your right hand,
near you it shall not come.
You need simply watch;
the punishment of the wicked you will see.
You have the LORD for your refuge;
you have made the Most High your stronghold.
No evil shall befall you,
no affliction come near your tent.
For God commands the angels
to guard you in all your ways.
With their hands they support you,
lest you strike your foot against a stone.
You shall tread upon the asp and the viper,
trample the lion and the dragon.

Whoever clings to me I will deliver;
whoever knows my name I will set on high.
All who call upon me I will answer;
I will be with them in distress;

I will deliver them and give them honor.
With length of days I will satisfy them
and show them my saving power.

E   Psalm 121

I raise my eyes toward the mountains.
From where will my help come?
My help comes from the LORD,
the maker of heaven and earth.
God will not allow your foot to slip;
your guardian does not sleep.
Truly, the guardian of Israel
never slumbers nor sleeps.

The LORD is your guardian;
the LORD is your shade
at your right hand.
By day the sun cannot harm you,
nor the moon by night.
The LORD will guard you from all evil,
will always guard your life.
The LORD will guard your coming and going
both now and forever.

F   1 John 4:16

We have come to know and to believe in the love
    God has for us.
    God is love, and whoever, remains in love
    remains in God and God in him.

G   Revelation 21:1-5a, 6-7

God our Father is the God of newness and life; it is his desire
that we should come to share his life with him.

I, John, saw a new heaven and a new earth.
The former heaven and the former earth had passed
   away,
   and the sea was no more.
I also saw the holy city, a new Jerusalem,
   coming down out of heaven from God,
   prepared as a bride adorned for her husband.
I heard a loud voice from the throne saying,
   "Behold, God's dwelling is with the human race.
God will dwell with them and they will be his
   people
   and God himself will always be with them as their
   God.
He will wipe every tear from their eyes,
   and there shall be no more death or mourning,
   wailing or pain,
   for the old order has passed away."

The One who sat on the throne said,
   "Behold, I make all things new.
I am the Alpha and the Omega,
   the beginning and the end.
To the thirsty I will give a gift
   from the spring of life-giving water.
The victor will inherit these gifts,
   and I shall be his God,
   and he will be my son."

H   Matthew 25:1-13

Jesus bids us be prepared for our ultimate destiny, which is eternal life.

Jesus spoke this parable to his disciples:
   "The kingdom of heaven will be like ten virgins
   who took their lamps and went out to meet the
      bridegroom.
Five of them were foolish and five were wise.
The foolish ones, when taking their lamps,
   brought no oil with them,
   but the wise brought flasks of oil with their lamps.
Since the bridegroom was long delayed,
   they all became drowsy and fell asleep.
At midnight, there was a cry,
   'Behold, the bridegroom! Come out to meet him!'
Then all those virgins got up and trimmed their
      lamps.
The foolish ones said to the wise,
   'Give us some of your oil,
   for our lamps are going out.'
But the wise ones replied,
   'No, for there may not be enough for us and you.
   Go instead to the merchants
   and buy some for yourselves.'
While they went off to buy it, the bridegroom came
   and those who were ready went into the wedding
      feast with him.
Then the door was locked.
Afterwards the other virgins came and said,
   'Lord, Lord, open the door for us!'
But he said in reply, 'Amen, I say to you,
   I do not know you.'
Therefore, stay awake,
   for you know neither the day nor the hour.''

I   Luke 22:39-46

Jesus is alive to our pain and sorrow, because faithfulness to his Father's will cost him life itself.

Then going out, Jesus went, as was his custom,
    to the Mount of Olives,
    and the disciples followed him.
When he arrived at the place he said to them,
    "Pray that you may not undergo the test."
After withdrawing about a stone's throw from
    them and kneeling,
    Jesus prayed, saying, "Father, if you are will-
    ing,
    take this cup away from me;
    still, not my will but yours be done."
And to strengthen him an angel from heaven
    appeared to him.
Jesus was in such agony and he prayed so
    fervently
    that his sweat became like drops of blood
    falling on the ground.
When he rose from prayer and returned to his
    disciples,
    he found them sleeping from grief.
He said to them, "Why are you sleeping?
Get up and pray that you may not undergo the
    test."

J   Luke 23:44-49

Jesus' death is witnessed by his friends.

It was now about noon and darkness came over the
    whole land
  until three in the afternoon
  because of an eclipse of the sun.
Then the veil of the temple was torn down the
    middle.
Jesus cried out in a loud voice,
  "Father, into your hands I commend my spirit";
  and when he had said this he breathed his last.
The centurion who witnessed what had happened
    glorified God and said,
  "This man was innocent beyond doubt."
When all the people who had gathered for this
    spectacle saw what had happened,
  they returned home beating their breasts;
  but all his acquaintances stood at a distance,
  including the women who had followed him from
    Galilee
  and saw these events.

K   Luke 24:1-8

Jesus is alive; he gives us eternal life with the Father.

At daybreak on the first day of the week
   the women took the spices they had prepared
   and went to the tomb.
They found the stone rolled away from the tomb;
   but when they entered,
   they did not find the body of the Lord Jesus.
While they were puzzling over this, behold,
   two men in dazzling garments appeared to them.
The women were terrified and bowed their faces to
      the ground.
The men said to the women,
   "Why do you seek the living one among the dead?
He is not here, but he has been raised.
Remember what he said to you while he was still
      in Galilee,
   that the Son of Man must be handed over to
      sinners
   and be crucified, and rise on the third day."
And the women remembered his words.

L   John 6:37-40

Jesus will raise his own from death and give them eternal life.

Jesus said to the crowds:
> "Everything that the Father gives me will come
>   to me,
> and I will not reject anyone who comes to me,
> because I came down from heaven not to do my
>   own will
> but the will of the one who sent me.
And this is the will of the one who sent me,
> that I should not lose anything of what he gave me,
> but that I should raise it on the last day.
For this is the will of my Father,
> that all who see the Son and believe in him
> may have eternal life,
> and I shall raise them on the last day."

M   John 14:1-6, 23, 27

The love of Jesus can raise us up from the sorrow of death to the joy of eternal life.

Jesus said to his disciples:
  "Do not let your hearts be troubled.
You have faith in God; have faith also in me.
In my Father's house there are many dwelling
    places.
If there were not,
  would I have told you that I am going to prepare
    a place for you?
And if I go and prepare a place for you,
  I will come back again and take you to myself,
  so that where I am you also may be.
Where I am going you know the way."
Thomas said to him,
  "Master, we do not know where you are going;
  how can we know the way?"
Jesus said to him, "I am the way and the truth and
    the life.
No one comes to the Father except through me.
Whoever loves me will keep my word,
  and my Father will love him,
  and we will come to him
  and make our dwelling place with him.
Peace I leave with you; my peace I give to you.
Not as the world gives do I give it to you.
Do not let your hearts be troubled or afraid."

Litany of the Saints

93   When the condition of the dying person calls for the
use of brief forms of prayer, those who are present are encouraged to pray the litany of the saints—or at least some
of its invocations—for him or her. Special mention may be
made of the patron saints of the dying person, of the family, and of the parish. The litany may be said or sung in
the usual way. Other customary prayers may also be used.

A **Lord, have mercy**   Lord, have mercy
  Christ, have mercy   Christ, have mercy
  Lord, have mercy   Lord, have mercy

  Holy Mary, Mother of God   pray for him/ her
  Holy angels of God   pray for him/ her
  Abraham, our father in faith   pray for him/ her
  David, leader of God's people   pray for him/ her
  All holy patriarchs and prophets   pray for him/ her

  Saint John the Baptist   pray for him/ her
  Saint Joseph   pray for him/ her
  Saint Peter and Saint Paul   pray for him/ her
  Saint Andrew   pray for him/ her
  Saint John   pray for him/ her
  Saint Mary Magdalene   pray for him/ her
  Saint Stephen   pray for him/ her
  Saint Ignatius   pray for him/ her
  Saint Lawrence   pray for him/ her
  Saint Perpetua and Saint Felicity   pray for him/ her
  Saint Agnes   pray for him/ her
  Saint Gregory   pray for him/ her
  Saint Augustine   pray for him/ her
  Saint Athanasius   pray for him/ her
  Saint Basil   pray for him/ her
  Saint Martin   pray for him/ her

Saint Benedict	pray for him/her
Saint Francis and Saint Dominic	pray for him/her
Saint Francis Xavier	pray for him/her
Saint John Vianney	pray for him/her
Saint Catherine	pray for him/her
Saint Teresa	pray for him/her

Other saints may be included here.

All holy men and women	pray for him/her
Lord, be merciful	Lord, save your people
From all evil	Lord, save your people
From every sin	Lord, save your people
From Satan's power	Lord, save your people
At the moment of death	Lord, save your people
From everlasting death	Lord, save your people
On the day of judgment	Lord, save your people
By your coming as man	Lord, save your people
By your suffering and cross	Lord, save your people
By your death and rising to new life	Lord, save your people
By your return in glory to the Father	Lord, save your people
By your gift of the Holy Spirit	Lord, save your people
By your coming again in glory	Lord, save your people
Be merciful to us sinners	Lord, hear our prayer
Bring N. to eternal life, first promised to him/her in baptism	Lord, hear our prayer
Raise N. on the last day, for he/she has eaten the bread of life	Lord, hear our prayer

Let **N.** share in your glory,
  for he/she has shared
  in your suffering and
    death   Lord, hear our prayer
Jesus, Son of the living
  God   Lord, hear our prayer

Christ, hear us   Christ, hear us
Lord Jesus,
  hear our prayer   Lord Jesus, hear our prayer

B   A brief form of the litany may be prayed. Other saints may
be added, including the patron saints of the dying person,
of the family, and of the parish; saints to whom the dying
person may have a special devotion may also be included.

Holy Mary, Mother of God   pray for him/her
Holy angels of God   pray for him/her
Saint John the Baptist   pray for him/her
Saint Joseph   pray for him/her
Saint Peter and Saint Paul   pray for him/her

    Other saints may be included here.

All holy men and women   pray for him/her

PRAYER OF COMMENDATION

94   When the moment of death seems near, some of the following prayers may be said:

A **Go forth, Christian soul, from this world**
in the name of God the almighty Father,
who created you,
in the name of Jesus Christ, Son of the living God,
who suffered for you,
in the name of the Holy Spirit,
who was poured out upon you,
go forth, faithful Christian.

May you live in peace this day,
may your home be with God in Zion,
with Mary, the virgin Mother of God,
with Joseph, and all the angels and saints.

B **I commend you, my dear brother /sister, to almighty**
  God,
and entrust you to your Creator.
May you return to him
who formed you from the dust of the earth.
May holy Mary, the angels, and all the saints
come to meet you as you go forth from this life.
May Christ who was crucified for you
bring you freedom and peace.
May Christ who died for you
admit you into his garden of paradise.
May Christ, the true Shepherd,
acknowledge you as one of his flock.
May he forgive all your sins,
and set you among those he has chosen.
May you see your Redeemer face to face,
and enjoy the vision of God for ever.

  ℟. **Amen.**

C Welcome your servant, Lord, into the place of salvation which because of your mercy he/she rightly hoped for.

℟. Amen.

or:

℟. Lord, save your people.

Deliver your servant, Lord, from every distress. ℟.

Deliver your servant, Lord, as you delivered Noah from the flood. ℟.

Deliver your servant, Lord, as you delivered Abraham from Ur of the Chaldees. ℟.

Deliver your servant, Lord, as you delivered Job from his sufferings. ℟.

Deliver your servant, Lord, as you delivered Moses from the hand of the Pharaoh. ℟.

Deliver your servant, Lord, as you delivered Daniel from the den of lions. ℟.

Deliver your servant, Lord, as you delivered the three young men from the fiery furnace. ℟.

Deliver your servant, Lord, as you delivered Susanna from her false accusers. ℟.

Deliver your servant, Lord, as you delivered David from the attacks of Saul and Goliath. ℟.

Deliver your servant, Lord, as you delivered Peter and Paul from prison. ℟.

Deliver your servant, Lord, through Jesus our Savior, who suffered death for us and gave us eternal life. ℟.

D Lord Jesus Christ, Savior of the world,
we pray for your servant N.,
and commend him/her to your mercy.
For his/her sake you came down from heaven;
receive him/her now into the joy of your kingdom.

For though he/she has sinned,
he/she has not denied the Father, the Son,
and the Holy Spirit,
but has believed in God
and has worshipped his/her Creator.

R⁊. Amen.

E The following antiphon may be said or sung:

Hail, holy Queen, Mother of mercy,
hail, our life, our sweetness, and our hope.
To you we cry, the children of Eve;
to you we send up our sighs,
mourning and weeping in this land of exile.
Turn, then, most gracious advocate,
your eyes of mercy toward us;
lead us home at last
and show us the blessed fruit of your womb, Jesus:
O clement, O loving, O sweet Virgin Mary.

Prayer after Death

95 When death has occurred, one or more of the following prayers may be said:

A Saints of God, come to his/her aid!
Come to meet him/her, angels of the Lord!

R⁊. Receive his/her soul and present him/her
to God the Most High.

May Christ, who called you, take you to himself;
may angels lead you to Abraham's side. ℟.

Give him/her eternal rest, O Lord,
and may your light shine on him/her for ever. ℟.

The following prayer is added:

Let us pray.

All-powerful and merciful God,
we commend to you N., your servant.
In your mercy and love,
blot out the sins he/she has committed through
  human weakness.
In this world he/she has died:
let him/her live with you for ever.

We ask this through Christ our Lord.

℟. Amen.

B   Psalm 130

℟. My soul hopes in the Lord.

Out of the depths I call to you, LORD;
Lord, hear my cry!
May your ears be attentive
to my cry for mercy. ℟.

I wait with longing for the LORD,
my soul waits for his word.
My soul looks for the Lord
more than sentinels for daybreak. ℟.

For with the LORD is kindness,
with him is full redemption,
And God will redeem Israel
from all their sins. ℟.

The following prayer is added:

Let us pray.

**God of faithfulness,
in your wisdom you have called you servant N.
   out of this world;
release him/her from the bonds of sin,
and welcome him/her into your presence,
so that he/she may enjoy eternal light and peace
and be raised up in glory with all your saints.**

We ask this through Christ our Lord.

℟. **Amen.**

C   Psalm 23

℟. **Lord, remember me in your kingdom.**

**The LORD is my shepherd;
there is nothing I lack.
In green pastures you let me graze;
to safe waters you lead me;
you restore my strength.** ℟.

**You guide me along the right path
for the sake of your name.
Even when I walk through a dark valley,
I fear no harm for you are at my side;
your rod and staff give me courage.** ℟.

**You set a table before me
as my enemies watch;
You anoint my head with oil;
my cup overflows.** ℟.

**Only goodness and love will pursue me
all the days of my life;
I will dwell in the house of the LORD
for years to come.** ℟.

The following prayer is added:

Let us pray.

**Lord, in our grief we turn to you.
Are you not the God of love
who open your ears to all?**

**Listen to our prayers for your servant N.,
whom you have called out of this world:
lead him /her to your kingdom of light and peace
and count him /her among the saints in glory.**

We ask this through Christ our Lord.

℞. **Amen.**

D **Holy Lord, almighty and eternal God,
hear our prayers for your servant N.,
whom you have summoned out of this world.
Forgive his /her sins and failings
and grant him /her a place of refreshment, light,
and peace.**

**Let him /her pass unharmed through the gates
of death
to dwell with the blessed in light,
as you promised to Abraham and his children
for ever.
Accept N. into your safekeeping
and on the great day of judgment
raise him /her up with all the saints
to inherit your eternal kingdom.**

We ask this through Christ our Lord.

℞. **Amen.**

E Into your hands, O Lord,
   we humbly entrust our brother/sister N.
   In this life you embraced him/her with your
      tender love;
   deliver him/her now from every evil
   and bid him/her enter eternal rest.

   The old order has passed away:
   welcome him/her then into paradise,
   where there will be no sorrow, no weeping nor pain,
   but the fullness of peace and joy
   with your Son and the Holy Spirit
   for ever and ever.

   R̦. Amen.

F Into your hands, Father of mercies,
   we commend our brother/sister N.
   in the sure and certain hope
   that, together with all who have died in Christ,
   he/she will rise with him on the last day.

   [We give you thanks for the blessings
   which you bestowed upon N. in this life:
   they are signs to us of your goodness
   and of our fellowship with the saints in Christ.]

   Merciful Lord,
   turn toward us and listen to our prayers:
   open the gates of paradise to your servant
   and help us who remain
   to comfort one another with assurances of faith,
   until we all meet in Christ
   and are with you and with our brother/sister for ever.

   We ask this through Christ our Lord.

   R̦. Amen.

Prayer for the Family and Friends

96   One of the following prayers may be said:

Let us pray.

A   For the family and friends

**Father of mercies and God of all consolation,
you pursue us with untiring love
and dispel the shadow of death
with the bright dawn of life.**

**[Comfort your family in their loss and sorrow.
Be our refuge and our strength, O Lord,
and lift us from the depths of grief
into the peace and light of your presence.]**

**Your Son, our Lord Jesus Christ,
by dying has destroyed our death,
and by rising, restored our life.
Enable us therefore to press on toward him,
so that, after our earthly course is run,
he may reunite us with those we love,
when every tear will be wiped away.**

We ask this through Christ our Lord.

℞. **Amen.**

B   For the deceased person and for the family and friends

Lord Jesus, our Redeemer,
you willingly gave yourself up to death,
so that all might be saved and pass from death to life.
We humbly ask you to comfort your servants in
  their grief
and to receive N. **into the arms of your mercy.**
You alone are the Holy One,
you are mercy itself;
by dying you unlocked the gates of life
  for those who believe in you.
Forgive N. **his/ her sins,**
and grant him/ her a place of happiness, light,
  and peace
in the kingdom of your glory for ever and ever.

  ℟. **Amen.**

For the sake of the solace of those present the minister may
conclude these prayers by invoking God's blessing making
the sign of the cross on himself or herself, while saying:

May the Lord bless us,
protect us from all evil,
and bring us to everlasting life.

  ℟. **Amen.**

Or the minister may conclude with a symbolic gesture, for
example, signing the forehead of the deceased person with
the sign of the cross.

Chapter 6

PRAYERS AFTER DEATH

INTRODUCTION

Blessed are the sorrowing; they shall be consoled.

97   This rite provides a model of prayer that may be used when the minister first meets with the family following death. The rite follows a common pattern of reading, response, prayer, and blessing and may be adapted according to the circumstances.

98   The presence of the minister and the calming effect of familiar prayers can comfort the mourners as they begin to face their loss. When the minister is present with the family at the time death occurs, this rite can be used as a quiet and prayerful response to the death. In other circumstances, for example, in the case of sudden or unexpected death, this form of prayer can be the principal part of the first pastoral visit of the minister.

99   The initial pastoral visit can be important as the first tangible expression of the community's support for the mourners. A minister unfamiliar with the family or the deceased person can learn a great deal on this occasion about the needs of the family and about the life of the deceased. The minister may also be able to form some preliminary judgments to help the family in planning the funeral rites. If circumstances allow, some first steps in the planning may take place at this time.

OUTLINE OF THE RITE

INTRODUCTION
  Invitation to Prayer
  Reading
  The Lord's Prayer
  Concluding Prayer
  Blessing

INVITATION TO PRAYER

100 Using one of the following greetings, or in similar words, the minister greets those present.

A **In this moment of sorrow**
   the Lord is in our midst
   and consoles us with his word:
   Blessed are the sorrowful; they shall be comforted.

B **Praised be God, the Father of our Lord Jesus Christ,**
   the Father of mercies,
   and the God of all consolation!
   He comforts us in all our afflictions
   and thus enables us to comfort those who grieve
   with the same consolation
   we have received from him.

The minister then invites those present to pray in silence.

READING

101 The minister or one of those present proclaims the reading. A reading from Part IV, p. 106, or one of the following may be used.

A   Matthew 18:19-20

Jesus said to his disciples:
    "Amen, I say to you, if two of you agree on earth
    about anything for which they are to pray,
    it shall be granted to them by my heavenly Father.
For where two or three are gathered together in my
        name,
    there am I in the midst of them."

B   John 11:21-24

Martha said to Jesus,
    "Lord, if you had been here,
    my brother would not have died.
But even now I know that whatever you ask of God,
    God will give you."
Jesus said to Martha,
    "Your brother will rise."
Martha said to Jesus,
    "I know he will rise,
    in the resurrection on the last day."
Jesus told her,
    "I am the resurrection and the life;
    those who believe in me, even if they die, will
        live,
    and those who live and believe in me will never
        die.
    Do you believe this?"
Martha said to him, "Yes, Lord.
    I have come to believe that you are the Messiah,
        the Son of God,
    the one who is coming into the world."

C   Luke 20:35-38

Jesus said to them,
   "Those who are deemed worthy to attain to the
      coming age
   and to the resurrection of the dead
   neither marry nor are given in marriage.
They can no longer die,
   for they are like angels;
   and they are the children of God
   because they are the ones who will rise.
That the dead will rise
   even Moses made known in the passage about
      the bush,
   when he called out 'Lord,'
   the God of Abraham, the God of Isaac, and the
      God of Jacob;
   and he is not God of the dead, but of the living,
   for to him all are alive."

THE LORD'S PRAYER

102 Using one of the following invitations, or in similar
words, the minister invites those present to pray the Lord's
Prayer.

A With God there is mercy and fullness of redemption;
let us pray as Jesus taught us:

B Let us pray for the coming of the kingdom as Jesus
taught us:

   All:
   Our Father. . . .

CONCLUDING PRAYERS

103   A prayer for the deceased person is then said. This
prayer may be followed by a prayer for the mourners.

For the deceased person: The minister says the following prayer
or one of those provided in no. 107.

Holy Lord, almighty and eternal God,
hear our prayers for your servant N.,
whom you have summoned out of this world.
Forgive his/ her sins and failings
and grant him/ her a place of refreshment, light,
    and peace.
Let him/ her pass unharmed through the gates of
    death
to dwell with the blessed in light,
as you promised to Abraham and his children
    for ever.
Accept N. into your safekeeping
and on the great day of judgment
raise him/ her up with all the saints
to inherit your eternal kingdom.

We ask this through Christ our Lord.

R7. **Amen.**

For the mourners: The minister may then say the following
prayer or one of those provided in no. 108.

Father of mercies and God of all consolation,
you pursue us with untiring love
and dispel the shadow of death
with the bright dawn of life.

[**Comfort your family in their loss and sorrow.**
Be our refuge and our strength, O Lord,
and lift us from the depths of grief
into the peace and light of your presence.]

Your Son, our Lord Jesus Christ,
by dying has destroyed our death,
and by rising, restored our life.
Enable us therefore to press on toward him,
so that, after our earthly course is run,
he may reunite us with those we love,
when every tear will be wiped away.

We ask this through Christ our Lord.

℞. Amen.

BLESSING

104   The minister says:

Blessed are those who have died in the Lord;
let them rest from their labors
   for their good deeds go with them.

A gesture, for example, signing the forehead of the deceased
with the sign of the cross, may accompany the following
words.

Eternal rest grant unto him/her, O Lord.

℞. And let perpetual light shine upon him/her.

May he/she rest in peace.

℞. Amen.

May his/her soul and the souls of all the faithful
   departed,
through the mercy of God, rest in peace.

℞. Amen.

A lay minister invokes God's blessing and signs himself or herself with the sign of the cross, saying:

**May the love of God and the peace of the Lord Jesus Christ
bless and console us
and gently wipe every tear from our eyes:
in the name of the Father,
and of the Son, and of the Holy Spirit.**

℟. **Amen.**

Part IV
A SELECTION OF READINGS, RESPONSES, AND VERSES FROM SACRED SCRIPTURE

A SELECTION OF READINGS, RESPONSES, AND VERSES FROM SACRED SCRIPTURE

105   The following readings may be used in the visitation of the sick, or when praying for the sick. The selection should be made according to pastoral need, and special attention should be given to the physical and spiritual condition of the sick persons for whom the readings are used. Certain readings are indicated as more suitable for the dying.

Old Testament Readings

A **A reading from the book of Job**   7:1-4, 6-11

Remember that our life is like the wind, and yet we are destined for eternal life with God.

Job spoke, saying:
"Is not human life on earth a drudgery?
  Are not their days those of hirelings?
They are slaves who long for the shade,
  hirelings who wait for their wages.
So I have been assigned months of misery,
  and troubled nights have been allotted to me.
If in bed I say, 'When shall I arise?'
  then the night drags on;
  I am filled with restlessness until the dawn.

"My days are swifter than a weaver's shuttle;
  they come to an end without hope.
Remember that my life is like the wind;
  I shall not see happiness again.
The eye that now sees me shall no more behold me;
  as you look at me, I shall be gone.
As a cloud dissolves and vanishes,
  so they who go down to the netherworld
    shall come up no more.
They shall not again return to their houses;
  their places shall know them no more.

"My own utterance I will not restrain;
  I will speak in the anguish of my spirit;
  I will complain in the bitterness of my soul."

The word of the Lord.

For the dying

B **A reading from the book of Job** 19:23-27

I know that my Redeemer lives.

Job spoke, saying:
"Oh, would that my words were written down!
    Would that they were inscribed in a record:
that with an iron chisel and with lead
    they were cut in the rock forever!
But as for me, I know that my Vindicator lives,
    and that he will at last stand forth upon the dust;
whom I myself shall see."

The word of the Lord.

C **A reading from the book
of the prophet Isaiah** 61:1-3a

The spirit of the Lord is upon me to comfort all who mourn.

The spirit of the Lord GOD is upon me,
    because the LORD has anointed me;
he has sent me to bring glad tidings to the lowly,
    to heal the brokenhearted,
to proclaim liberty to the captives
    and release to the prisoners,
to announce a year of favor from the LORD
    and a day of vindication by our God,
    to comfort all who mourn;
to place on those who mourn in Zion
    a diadem instead of ashes,
to give them oil of gladness in place of mourning,
    a glorious mantle instead of a listless spirit.

The word of the Lord.

Or:

Job 7:12-21—*What are we, that you make much of us?*

Wisdom 9:1a, 9-18—*Who could know your counsel? We ask to share in God's wisdom.*

Isaiah 35:1-10—*Strengthen the feeble hands.*

Isaiah 52:13–53:12—*He bore our sufferings himself.*

NEW TESTAMENT READINGS

Easter Season

A **A reading from the Acts of the Apostles**   3:11-16

Faith in Jesus has given this man perfect health.

As the beggar who had been cured clung to Peter and John,
  all the people hurried in amazement toward them
  in the portico called "Solomon's Portico."
When Peter saw this, he addressed the people,
  "You Israelites, why are you amazed at this,
  and why do you look so intently at us
  as if we had made him walk by our own power or piety?
The God of Abraham, the God of Isaac, and the God of Jacob,
  the God of our ancestors, has glorified his servant Jesus
  whom you handed over and denied in Pilate's presence,
  when Pilate had decided to release him.
You denied the Holy and Righteous One
  and asked that a murderer be released to you.

The author of life you put to death,
    but God raised him from the dead; of this we are
        witnesses.
And by faith in the name of Jesus,
    this man, whom you see and know, the name of
        Jesus has made strong,
    and the faith that comes through it
    has given this man perfect health,
    in the presence of all of you.''

The word of the Lord.

B **A reading from the Acts of the Apostles**   4:8-12

*There is no other name but the name of Jesus by which we are
saved.*

Peter, filled with the Holy Spirit, said:
    ''Leaders of the people and elders:
    If we are being examined today
    about a good deed done to a man lame from birth,
    namely, by what means he was saved,
    then all of you and all the people of Israel should
        know
    that it was in the name of Jesus Christ the Nazo-
        rean
    whom you crucified, whom God raised from the
        dead;
    in his name this man stands before you healed.
Jesus is the stone rejected by you, the builders,
    which has become the cornerstone.
There is no salvation through anyone else,
    nor is there any other name under heaven
    given to the human race by which we are to be
        saved.''

The word of the Lord.

C **A reading from the Acts of the Apostles** 13:32-39

The one whom God raised from the dead will never see corruption of the flesh.

Paul said:

"We ourselves are proclaiming this good news to
   you
  that what God promised our ancestors
  he has brought to fulfillment for us, their children,
    by raising up Jesus,
  as it is written in the second psalm,
 'You are my son; this day I have begotten you.'
And that God raised Jesus from the dead never to
   return to corruption
  he declared in this way,
 'I shall give you the benefits assured to David.'
That is why he also says in another psalm,
 'You will not suffer your holy one to see corruption.'
Now David, after he had served the will of God
   in his lifetime,
  fell asleep, was gathered to his ancestors, and did
   see corruption.
But the one whom God raised up did not see corruption.
You must know, my brothers and sisters
  that through Jesus forgiveness of sins is being
   proclaimed to you,
  and in regard to everything from which you could
   not be justified under the law of Moses,
  in Jesus every believer is justified."

                  The word of the Lord.

Or:

Acts 3:1-10—*In the name of Jesus, stand up and walk.*

Other Seasons

D **A reading from the letter of Paul
to the Romans** 8:14-17

If we suffer with him, we will be glorified with him.

Brothers and sisters:
For those who are led by the Spirit of God are chil-
dren of God.
For you did not receive a spirit of slavery to fall
back into fear,
but you received a spirit of adoption,
through which we cry, Abba, ''Father!''
The Spirit itself bears witness with our spirit
that we are children of God,
and if children, then heirs,
heirs of God and joint heirs with Christ,
if only we suffer with Christ
so that we may also be glorified with him.

The word of the Lord.

E **A reading from the letter of Paul
to the Romans** 8:31b-35, 37-39

Nothing can come between us and the love of Christ.

Brothers and sisters:
If God is for us, who can be against us?
God did not spare his own Son
  but handed him over for us all,
  will God not also give us everything else along
    with his Son?
Who will bring a charge against God's chosen ones?
It is God who acquits us.
Who will condemn?
It is Christ Jesus who died, rather, was raised,
  who also is at the right hand of God,
  who indeed intercedes for us.
Who will separate us from the love of Christ?
Will anguish, or distress or persecution, or famine,
  or nakedness, or peril, or the sword?

No, in all these things, we conquer overwhelmingly
  through Christ Jesus who loved us.
For I am convinced that neither death, nor life,
  nor angels, nor principalities,
  nor present things, nor future things,
  nor powers, nor height, nor depth,
  nor any other creature will be able to separate us
  from the love of God in Christ Jesus our Lord.

The word of the Lord.

F **A reading from the letter of Paul
to the Romans** 12:1-2

*All our lives, even our suffering and pain, are caught up in the
offering of Christ in obedience to the will of our Father.*

**I urge you, brothers and sisters, by the mercies of
God**
  to offer your bodies as a living sacrifice,
  holy and pleasing to God, your spiritual worship.
Do not conform yourselves to this age
  but be transformed by the renewal of your mind,
  that you may discern what is the will of God,
  what is good and pleasing and perfect.

                        The word of the Lord.

Or:

Romans 8:18-27—*We groan while we wait for the redemption
of our bodies. The Spirit enables us to pray in our suffering.*

1 Corinthians 1:18-25—*God's weakness is stronger than human
strength.*

For the dying

G **A reading from the first letter of Paul
to the Corinthians**   15:1-4

The death and resurrection of Christ, the basis of our faith.

Brothers and sisters:
  **Now I am reminding you of the gospel I preached
    to you,**
    **which you indeed received and in which you also
    stand.**
**Through it you are also being saved, if you hold
    fast to the word I preached to you,**
    unless you believed in vain.
**For I handed on to you as of first importance what
    I also received:**
    **that Christ died for our sins in accordance with
    the scriptures;**
    that he was buried;
    **that he was raised on the third day
    in accordance with the scriptures.**

                              The word of the Lord.

For the dying

H **A reading from the second letter of Paul
to the Corinthians** 5:1, 6-10

We have an everlasting home in heaven.

Brothers and sisters:
We know that if our earthly dwelling, a tent,
  should be destroyed,
  we have a building from God,
  a dwelling not made with hands,
  eternal in heaven.

We are always courageous,
  although we know that while we are at home in
    the body
  we are away from the Lord,
  for we walk by faith, not by sight.
Yet we are courageous,
  and we would rather leave the body and go home
    to the Lord.
Therefore, we aspire to please the Lord,
  whether we are at home or away.
For we must all appear before the judgment seat
    of Christ,
  so that each may receive recompense,
  according to what was done in the body, whether
    good or evil.

                    The word of the Lord.

Or:

1 Corinthians 15:12-20—*Christ has been raised from the dead;
through him has come the resurrection of us all.*

I **A reading from the letter of Paul
to the Colossians** 1:22-29

*In my flesh I fill up what is lacking in the sufferings of Christ
for the sake of his body.*

Brothers and sisters:
Christ Jesus has now reconciled you
  in his fleshly body through his death,
  to present you holy, without blemish,
  and irreproachable before him,
  provided that you persevere in the faith,
  firmly grounded, stable,
  and not shifting from the hope of the gospel that
    you heard,
  which has been preached to every creature under
    heaven,
  of which I, Paul, am a minister.

Now I, Paul rejoice in my sufferings for your sake,
  and in my flesh I am filling up
  what is lacking in the afflictions of Christ
  on behalf of his body, which is the church,
  of which I am a minister
  in accordance with God's stewardship given to me
  to bring to completion for you the word of God,
  the mystery hidden from ages and from genera-
    tions past.
But now it has been manifested to his holy ones,
  to whom God chose to make known the riches of
    the glory
  of this mystery among the Gentiles;
  it is Christ in you, the hope for glory.
It is Christ whom we proclaim,
  admonishing everyone and teaching everyone
    with all wisdom,

that we may present everyone perfect in Christ.
For this I labor and struggle,
  in accord with the exercise of his power working
    within me.

The word of the Lord.

J A reading from the letter of James   5:13-16

This prayer, made in faith, will save the sick person.

Are any among you suffering?
They should pray.
Are any in good spirits?
They should sing songs of praise.
Are any among you sick?
They should summon the presbyters of the church,
  and they should pray over the sick
  and anoint the sick with oil in the name of the
    Lord.
  The prayer of faith will save the sick,
  and the Lord will raise them up.
If they have committed any sins, they will be for-
  given.

Therefore, confess your sins to one another
  and pray for one another, that you may be healed.
The fervent prayer of a righteous person is very
  powerful.
Elijah was a human being like us;
  yet he prayed earnestly that it might not rain,
  and for three years and six months it did not rain
    upon the land.
Then Elijah prayed again, and the sky gave rain
  and the earth produced its fruit.

The word of the Lord.

K **A reading from the first letter of Peter** 1:3-9

You will rejoice even though for a short time you must suffer.

Blessed be the God and Father of our Lord Jesus
    Christ,
  who in his great mercy gave us a new birth to a
    living hope
  through the resurrection of Jesus Christ from the
    dead,
  to an inheritance that is imperishable, undefiled,
    and unfading,
  kept in heaven for you
  who by the power of God are safeguarded through
    faith,
  to a salvation that is ready to be revealed in the
    final time.
In this you rejoice, although now for a little while
  you may have to suffer through various trials,
  so that the genuineness of your faith,
  more precious than gold that is perishable even
    though tested by fire,
  may prove to be for praise, glory, and honor
  at the revelation of Jesus Christ.
Although you have not seen him you love him;
  even though you do not see him now yet you be-
    lieve in him,
  you rejoice with an indescribable and glorious joy,
  as you attain the goal of faith, the salvation of
    your souls.

                              The word of the Lord.

L **A reading from the first letter of John** 3:1-2

What we shall be has not yet been revealed.

Beloved:
See what love the Father has bestowed on us
that we may be called the children of God.
Yet so we are.
The reason the world does not know us
is that it did not know the Son.
Beloved, we are God's children now;
what we shall be has not yet been revealed.
We do know that when it is revealed we shall be
like God,
for we shall see God as he is.

The word of the Lord.

M **A reading from the book of Revelation** 21:1-7

There will be no more death or mourning, sadness or pain.

I, John, saw a new heaven and a new earth.
The former heaven and the former earth had passed
    away,
    and the sea was no more.
I also saw the holy city, a new Jerusalem,
    coming down out of heaven from God,
    prepared as a bride adorned for her husband.
I heard a loud voice from the throne saying,
    "Behold, God's dwelling is with the human race.
God will dwell with them and they will be his
    people
    and God himself will always be with them as their
    God.
He will wipe every tear from their eyes,
    and there shall be no more death or mourning,
    wailing or pain,
    for the old order has passed away."

The one who sat on the throne said,
    "Behold, I make all things new."
Then he said, "Write these words down,
    for they are trustworthy and true."
He said to me, "They are accomplished.
I am the Alpha and the Omega, the beginning and
    the end.
To the thirsty I will give a gift
    from the spring of the life-giving water.
Those who are victorious will inherit these gifts,
    and I shall be their God,
    and they will be my children."

The word of the Lord.

Or:

Hebrews 4:14-16; 5:7-9—*Jesus identified himself with us totally; he suffered, and through his suffering discovered the will of the Father.*

For the dying

N **A reading from the book of Revelation** 22:17, 20-21

Come, Lord Jesus!

The Spirit and the bride say, "Come."
Let the hearer say, "Come."
Let the one who thirsts come forward,
   and the one who wants it receive the gift of life-giving water.

The one who gives this testimony says,
  "Yes, I am coming soon."
Amen! Come, Lord Jesus!
The grace of the Lord Jesus be with you all.

                        The word of the Lord.

RESPONSORIAL PSALMS

A   Isaiah 38

The cry of a suffering person and joy in God's strength.

R̞. (17b) **You saved my life, O Lord; I shall
not die.**

**Once I said,
"In the noontime of life I must depart!
To the gates of the nether world I shall be consigned
for the rest of my years."** R̞.

**I said, "I shall see the LORD no more
in the land of the living.
No longer shall I behold my fellow men
among those who dwell in the world."** R̞.

**My dwelling, like a shepherd's tent,
is struck down and borne away from me;
You have folded up my life, like a weaver
who severs the last thread.** R̞.

**Those live whom the LORD protects;
yours is the life of my spirit.
You have given me health and life;
thus is my bitterness transformed into peace.** R̞.

B   Psalm 6

A suffering person who cries to God for strength.

℟. **(3a) Have mercy on me, Lord; my strength
    is gone.**

**Do not reprove me in your anger, LORD
nor punish me in your wrath.
Have pity on me, LORD, for I am weak;
heal me, LORD, for my bones are trembling.
In utter terror is my soul—** ℟.

**And you, LORD, how long . . . ?
Turn, LORD, save my life;
in your mercy rescue me.
For who among the dead remembers you?
Who praises you in Sheol?** ℟.

**Away from me, all who do evil!
The LORD has heard weeping.
The LORD has heard my prayer;
the LORD takes up my plea.** ℟.

C   Psalm 25

A prayer for forgiveness and salvation.

℟. (1) **To you, O Lord, I lift my soul.**

**Make known to me your ways, LORD;
teach me your paths.
Guide me in your truth and teach me,
for you are God my savior.
For you I wait all the long day.** ℟.

**Remember your compassion and love, O LORD;
for they are ages old.
Remember no more the sins of my youth;
remember me only in light of your love.** ℟.

**Good and upright is the LORD,
who shows sinners the way,
Guides the humble rightly,
and teaches the humble the way.** ℟.

**All the paths of the LORD are faithful love
toward those who honor the covenant demands.
The counsel of the LORD belongs to the faithful;
the covenant instructs them.** ℟.

**My eyes are ever upon the LORD,
who frees my feet from the snare.
Look upon me, have pity on me,
for I am alone and afflicted.** ℟.

D   Psalm 34

God is the salvation of those who trust in him.

℟. **(19a) The Lord is near to broken hearts.**

Or:

℟. **(9a) Taste and see the goodness of the Lord.**

I will bless the LORD at all times;
praise shall be always in my mouth.
My soul will glory in the LORD
that the poor may hear and be glad. ℟.

Magnify the LORD with me;
let us exalt his name together.
I sought the LORD, who answered me,
delivered me from all my fears. ℟.

Look to God that you may be radiant with joy
and your faces may not blush for shame.
In my misfortune I called,
the LORD heard and saved me from all distress. ℟.

Fear the LORD, you holy ones;
nothing is lacking to those who fear him.
The powerful grow poor and hungry,
but those who seek the LORD lack no good thing. ℟.

Come, children, listen to me;
I will teach you the fear of the LORD.
Who among you loves life,
takes delight in prosperous days? ℟.

The LORD's face is against evildoers
to wipe out their memory from the earth.
The LORD is close to the brokenhearted,
saves those whose spirit is crushed. ℟.

E   Psalm 63

A prayer of desire to be with God.

℞. (2b) **My soul is thirsting for you, O Lord
    my God.**

**O God, you are my God—
for you I long!
For you my body yearns;
for you my soul thirsts,
Like a land parched, lifeless,
and without water.
So I look to you in the sanctuary
to see your power and glory.** ℞.

**For your love is better than life;
my lips offer you worship!
I will bless you as long as I live;
I will lift up my hands, calling on your name.
My soul shall savor the rich banquet of praise,
with joyous lips my mouth shall honor you!** ℞.

**When I think of you upon my bed,
through the night watches I will recall
That you indeed are my help,
and in the shadow of your wings I shout for joy.
My soul clings fast to you;
your right hand upholds me.** ℞.

F   Psalm 71

God is our hope in all our trials.

℟. (12b) **My God, come quickly to help me.**

Or:

℟. (23) **My lips, my very soul will shout for
joy: you have redeemed me!**

In you, LORD, I take refuge;
let me never be put to shame.
In your justice rescue me and deliver me;
listen to me and save me! ℟.

For you are my hope, Lord;
my trust, GOD, from my youth.
On you I depend since birth;
from my mother's womb you are my strength;
my hope in you never wavers. ℟.

My mouth shall be filled with your praise,
shall sing your glory every day.
Do not cast me aside in my old age;
as my strength fails, do not forsake me. ℟.

I will always hope in you
and add to all your praise.
My mouth shall proclaim your just deeds,
day by day your acts of deliverance. ℟.

G   Psalm 86

Prayer of those who are in distress.

℟. (1a) **Listen, Lord, and answer me.**

Or:

℟ . (15a and 16a) **God, you are merciful and
    kind; turn to me and have mercy.**

**Hear me, LORD, and answer me,
for I am poor and oppressed.
Preserve my life, for I am loyal;
save your servant who trusts in you.** ℟.

**You are my God; pity me, Lord;
to you I call all the day.
Gladden the soul of your servant;
to you, Lord, I lift up my soul.** ℟.

**Lord, you are kind and forgiving,
most loving to all who call on you.
LORD, hear my prayer;
listen to my cry for help.** ℟.

**Teach me, LORD, your way
that I may walk in your truth,
single-hearted and revering your name.** ℟.

**I will praise you with all my heart,
glorify your name forever, Lord my God.
Your love for me is great;
you have rescued me from the depths of Sheol.** ℟.

**But you, Lord, are a merciful and gracious God,
slow to anger, most loving and true.
Turn to me, have pity on me;
give your strength to your servant.** ℟.

H   Psalm 90

Our God is eternal, strong, with power to save us.

℞. (1) **In every age, O Lord, you have been our refuge.**

Before the mountains were born,
the earth and the world brought forth,
from eternity to eternity you are God. ℞.

But humans you return to dust,
saying, ''Return, you mortals!''
A thousand years in your eyes
are merely a yesterday,
Before a watch passes in the night. ℞.

They disappear like sleep at dawn;
they are like grass that dies.
It sprouts green in the morning;
by evening it is dry and withered. ℞.

Our life ebbs away under your wrath;
our years end like a sigh.
Seventy is the sum of our years,
or eighty, if we are strong. ℞.

Most of them are sorrow and toil;
they pass quickly, we are all but gone.
Teach us to count our days aright,
that we may gain wisdom of heart. ℞.

Fill us at daybreak with your love,
that all our days we may sing for joy.
Show your deeds to your servants,
your glory to their children. ℞.

I   Psalm 123

God is the hope of his people.

℟. **(2cd) Our eyes are fixed on the Lord, pleading for his mercy.**

**To you I raise my eyes
to you enthroned in heaven.
Yes, like the eyes of a servant
on the hand of his master.** ℟.

**Like the eyes of a maid
on the hand of her mistress,
So our eyes are on the LORD our God,
till we are shown favor.** ℟.

J   Psalm 143

A prayer for help in time of trouble.

℟. **(1a) O Lord, hear my prayer.**

Or:

℟. **(11a) For the sake of your name, O Lord,
save my life.**

**LORD, hear my prayer;
in your faithfulness listen to my pleading;
answer me in your justice.
Do not enter into judgment with your servant;
before you no living being can be just.** ℟.

**I remember the days of old;
I ponder all your deeds;
the works of your hands I recall.
I stretch out my hands to you;
I thirst for you like a parched land.** ℟.

**Teach me to do your will,
for you are my God.
May your kind spirit guide me
on ground that is level.** ℟.

Or:

Psalm 27:1, 4, 7-9a, 9b-10
℟. Put your hope in the Lord; take courage and be strong.

Psalm 42:2, 3, 5 and Psalm 43:3, 4, 5
℟. **(2)** Like a deer that longs for running streams, my soul longs for you, my God.

Psalm 103:1-2, 13-14, 15-16, 17-18
℟. Bless the Lord, O my soul.
or: The Lord is kind and merciful; slow to anger, and rich in compassion.

ALLELUIA VERSE AND VERSE BEFORE THE GOSPEL

A   Psalm 33:22

LORD, let you mercy be on us,
as we place our trust in you.

B   Matthew 5:4

Happy are they who mourn;
they shall be comforted.

C   Matthew 8:17

He bore our sickness,
and endured our suffering.

D   Matthew 11:28

Come to me, all you that labor and are burdened,
and I will give you rest, says the Lord.

E   2 Corinthians 1:3b-4a

Blessed be the Father of mercies and the God of all
   comfort,
who consoles us in all our afflictions.

F   Ephesians 1:3

Blessed be God, the Father of our Lord Jesus Christ,
for he has blessed us with every spiritual gift in
   Christ.

G   James 1:12

Blessed are they who stand firm when trials come;
when they have stood the test, they will win the
   crown of life.

GOSPEL READINGS

A **A reading from the holy gospel
according to Matthew**   5:1-12a

Rejoice and be glad, for your reward is great in heaven.

When Jesus saw the crowds, he went up the mountain,
  and after he had sat down, his disciples came to him.
He began to teach them, saying:
  "Blessed are the poor in spirit,
    for theirs is the kingdom of heaven.
  Blessed are they who mourn,
    for they will be comforted.
  Blessed are the meek,
    for they will inherit the land.
  Blessed are they who hunger and thirst for righteousness,
    for they will be satisfied.
  Blessed are the merciful,
    for they will be shown mercy.
  Blessed are the clean of heart,
    for they will see God.
  Blessed are the peacemakers,
    for they will be called children of God.
  Blessed are they who are persecuted for the sake
    of righteousness,
    for theirs is the kingdom of heaven.
  Blessed are you when they insult you and persecute you
    and utter every kind of evil against you falsely
    because of me.
  Rejoice and be glad,
    for your reward will be great in heaven."
                              The gospel of the Lord.

B **A reading from the holy gospel
according to Matthew** 8:1-4

If you wish to do so, you can cure me.

When Jesus came down from the mountain,
    great crowds followed him.
And then a leper approached, did him homage, and
        said,
    "Lord, if you wish, you can make me clean."
He stretched out his hand, touched him, and said,
    "I will do it. Be made clean."
His leprosy was cleansed immediately.
Then Jesus said to him, "See that you tell no one,
    but go show yourself to the priest,
    and offer the gift that Moses prescribed;
    that will be proof for them."

The gospel of the Lord.

C **A reading from the holy gospel
according to Matthew** 11:25-30

Come to me, all you who labor.

At that time Jesus responded:
    "I give praise to you, Father, Lord of heaven and
        earth,
    for although you have hidden these things
    from the wise and the learned
    you have revealed them to the childlike.
Yes, Father, such has been your gracious will.
All things have been handed over to me by my
        Father.

No one knows the Son except the Father,
  and no one knows the Father except the Son
  and anyone to whom the Son wishes to reveal
    him.''

''Come to me, all you who labor and are burdened,
  and I will give you rest.
Take my yoke upon you and learn for me,
  for I am meek and humble of heart;
  and you will find rest for yourselves.
For my yoke is easy, and my burden light.''

The gospel of the Lord.

D **A reading from the holy gospel**
  according to Matthew   15:29-31

Jesus heals large crowds.

Jesus walked by the Sea of Galilee,
  went up on the mountain, and sat down there.
Great crowds came to him,
  having with them those who were lame, or blind,
    or deformed, or mute,
  and many others.
They placed them at his feet, and Jesus cured them.
The crowds were amazed when they saw those who
    were mute speaking,
  those who were deformed made whole,
  those who were lame walking,
  those who were blind able to see,
  and they glorified the God of Israel.

The gospel of the Lord.

E **A reading from the holy gospel
according to Matthew**   25:31-40

*As often as you did it to the least of these who belong to me, you
did it to me.*

Jesus said to his disciples:
  "When the Son of Man comes in his glory,
  and all the angels with him,
  he will sit upon his glorious throne,
  and all the nations will be assembled before him.
And the Son of Man will separate them one from
    another,
  as a shepherd separates the sheep from the goats.
He will place the sheep on his right and the goats
    on his left.
Then the king will say to those on his right,
  'Come, you who are blessed by my Father.
Inherit the kingdom prepared for you from the foun-
    dation of the world.
For I was hungry and you gave me food,
  I was thirsty and you gave me drink,
  a stranger and you welcomed me,
  naked and you clothed me,
  ill and you cared for me,
  in prison and you visited me.'
Then the righteous will answer him and say,
  'Lord, when did we see you hungry and feed you,
  or thirsty and give you drink?
When did we see you a stranger and welcome you,
  or naked and clothe you?
When did we see you ill or in prison, and visit you?'
And the king will say to them in reply,

'Amen, I say to you, whatever you did
for one of the least of my brothers or sisters, you
  did for me.' "

The gospel of the Lord.

F A reading from the holy gospel
according to Luke   7:18b-23

Go tell John what you have seen.

John summoned two of his disciples and sent them
  to the Lord to ask,
  "Are you the one who is to come, or should we
  look for another?"
When the men came to the Lord, they said,
  "John the Baptist has sent us to you to ask,
  'Are you the one who is to come, or should we
  look for another?' "
At that time
  Jesus cured many of their diseases, sufferings, and
  evil spirits;
  he also granted sight to many who were blind.
And Jesus said to them in reply,
  "Go and tell John what you have seen and heard:
  those who are blind regain their sight,
  those who are lame walk,
  those with leprosy are cleansed,
  those who are deaf hear, the dead are raised.
  those poor have the good news proclaimed to
  them.
And blessed is the one who takes no offense at me."

The gospel of the Lord.

G **A reading from the holy gospel
according to Luke**   10:5-6, 8-9

Heal the sick, Jesus commanded his followers.

**Jesus said to the seventy-two disciples:
  "Into whatever house you enter, first say,
  'Peace to this household.'
If a peaceful person lives there,
  your peace will rest on that person;
  but if not, it will return to you.
Whatever town you enter and they welcome you,
  eat what is set before you,
  cure the sick in it and say to them,
  'The kingdom of God is at hand for you.'"**

                The gospel of the Lord.

For the dying

H **A reading from the holy gospel
according to John**   6:35-40

*It is the will of my Father that what he has given me will not
perish.*

**Jesus said to the crowds:
  "I am the bread of life;
  whoever comes to me will never hunger,
  and whoever believes in me will never thirst.
But I told you that although you have seen me,
  you do not believe.
Everything that the Father gives me will come to me,
  and I will not reject anyone who comes to me,
  because I came down from heaven not to do my
    own will
  but the will of the one who sent me.
And this is the will of the one who sent me,**

that I should not lose anything of what he gave me,
but that I should raise it on the last day.
For this is the will of my Father,
that all who see the Son and believe in him
may have eternal life,
and I shall raise them on the last day."

The gospel of the Lord.

For the dying

I **A reading from the holy gospel
according to John** 6:53-58

Whoever eats this bread has eternal life.

Jesus said to the Jews:
"Amen, amen, I say to you,
unless you eat the flesh of the Son of Man and
drink his blood,
you do not have life within you.
Those who eat my flesh and drink my blood
have eternal life,
and I will raise them on the last day.
For my flesh is true food,
and my blood is true drink.
Those who eat my flesh and drink my blood
remain in me and I in them.
Just as the living Father sent me
and I have life because of the Father,
so also the one who feeds on me will have life
because of me.
This is the bread that came down from heaven.
Unlike your ancestors who ate and still died,
whoever eats this bread will live forever."

The gospel of the Lord.

J **A reading from the holy gospel
according to John**   10:11-18

The good shepherd lays down his life for his sheep.

Jesus said to the Pharisees:
  "I am the good shepherd.
A good shepherd lays down his life for the sheep.
A hired man, who is not a shepherd
  and whose sheep are not his own,
    sees a wolf coming and leaves the sheep and runs
      away,
  and the wolf catches and scatters them.
This is because he works for pay and has no con-
  cern for the sheep.
I am the good shepherd,
  and I know mine and mine know me,
    just as the Father knows me and I know the Father;
  and I will lay down my life for the sheep.
I have other sheep that do not belong to this fold.
These also I must lead, and they will hear my voice,
  and there will be one flock, one shepherd.
This is why the Father loves me,
  because I lay down my life in order to take it up
    again.
No one takes it from me, but I lay it down on my
  own.
I have power to lay it down, and power to take it
  up again.
This command I have received from my Father."

                              The gospel of the Lord.

Or:

Matthew 8:5-17—*He bore our infirmities.*

Mark 2:1-12—*Seeing their faith, Jesus said to the sick man: Your sins are forgiven.*

Mark 10:46-52—*Jesus, Son of David, have mercy on me.*

Luke 10:25-37—*Who is my neighbor?*

Luke 12:35-44—*Happy are those whom the master finds watching when he returns.*

John 9:1-7—*The blind man has not sinned; it was to let God's work show forth in him.*

Part V
PRAYERS AND TEXTS
IN PARTICULAR
CIRCUMSTANCES

PRAYERS FOR THE DEAD AND MOURNERS

106   The following prayers for the dead and prayers for the mourners are for use in the various rites of Chapters five and six.

The prayers are grouped as follows:

Prayers for the Dead

107 The following prayers for the dead may be used in the various rites of Chapters five and six. The prayers should be chosen taking the character of the text into account as well as the place in the rite where it will occur. All of the prayers in this section end with the shorter conclusion.

1   General

**God of faithfulness,
in your wisdom you have called your servant N. out
  of this world;
release him/her from the bonds of sin,
and welcome him/her into your presence,
so that he/she may enjoy eternal light and peace
and be raised up in glory with all your saints.**

We ask this through Christ our Lord.

  R℣. **Amen.**

2   General

**Lord, in our grief we turn to you.
Are you not the God of love
who open your ears to all?**

**Listen to our prayers for your servant N.,
whom you have called out of this world:
lead him/her to your kingdom of light and peace
and count him/her among the saints of glory.**

We ask this through Christ our Lord.

  R℣. **Amen.**

3   General

**Holy Lord, almighty and eternal God,
hear our prayers for your servant N.,**

whom you have summoned out of this world.
Forgive his/her sins and failings
and grant him/her a place of refreshment, light,
  and peace.
Let him/her pass unharmed through the gates of
  death
to dwell with the blessed in light,
as you promised to Abraham and his children
  for ever.
Accept N. into your safekeeping
and on the great day of judgment
raise him/her up with all the saints
to inherit your eternal kingdom.

We ask this through Christ our Lord.

℞. **Amen.**

4   General

Into your hands, O Lord,
we humbly entrust our brother/sister N.
In this life you embraced him/her with your
  tender love;
deliver him/her now from every evil
and bid him/her enter eternal rest.

The old order has passed away:
welcome him/her then into paradise,
where there will be no sorrow, no weeping nor pain,
but the fullness of peace and joy
with your Son and the Holy Spirit
for ever and ever.

℞. **Amen.**

5   General

Almighty God and Father,
it is our certain faith
that your Son, who died on the cross, was raised
   from the dead,
the firstfruits of all who have fallen asleep.
Grant that through this mystery
your servant N., who has gone to his her rest in
   Christ,
may share in the joy of his resurrection.

We ask this through Christ our Lord.

   R℣. Amen.

6   General

O God,
glory of believers and life of the just,
by the death and resurrection of your Son, we are
   redeemed:
have mercy on your servant N.,
and make him/her worthy to share the joys of
   paradise,
for he/she believed in the resurrection of the dead.

We ask this through Christ our Lord.

   R℣. Amen.

7   General

Almighty God and Father,
by the mystery of the cross, you have made us
   strong;
by the sacrament of the resurrection
you have sealed us as your own.

Look kindly upon your servant N.,
now freed from the bonds of mortality,
and count him her among your saints in heaven.

We ask this through Christ our Lord.

℟. **Amen.**

8   General

God of loving kindness,
listen favorably to our prayers:
strengthen our belief that your Son has risen from
  the dead
and our hope that your servant N. will also rise
  again.

We ask this through Christ our Lord.

℟. **Amen.**

9   General

To you, O God, the dead do not die,
and in death our life is changed, not ended.
Hear our prayers
and command the soul of your servant N.
to dwell with Abraham, your friend,
and be raised at last on the great day of judgment.
In your mercy cleanse him/her of any sin
which he/she may have committed through human
  frailty.

We ask this through Christ our Lord.

℟. **Amen.**

10   General

Lord God, in whom all find refuge,
we appeal to your boundless mercy:
grant to the soul of your servant N.
a kindly welcome,
cleansing of sin,
release from the chains of death,
and entry into everlasting life.

We ask this through Christ our Lord.

℞. **Amen.**

11   General

God of all consolation,
open our hearts to your word,
so that, listening to it, we may comfort one another,
finding light in time of darkness
and faith in time of doubt.

We ask this through Christ our Lord.

℞. **Amen.**

12   General

O God,
to whom mercy and forgiveness belong,
hear our prayers on behalf of your servant N.,
whom you have called out of this world;
and because he/she put his/her hope and trust in
   you,
command that he/she be carried safely home to
   heaven
and come to enjoy your eternal reward.

We ask this through Christ our Lord.

℞. **Amen.**

13 General

O God,
in whom sinners find mercy and the saints find joy,
we pray to you for our brother/sister N.,
whose body we honor with Christian burial,
that he/she may be delivered from the bonds of
  death.
Admit him/her to the joyful company of your saints
and raise him/her on the last day
to rejoice in your presence for ever.

We ask this through Christ our Lord.

R̷. Amen.

14 One who worked in the service of the Gospel

Faithful God,
we humbly ask your mercy for your servant N.,
who worked so generously to spread the Good
  News:
grant him/her the reward of his/her labors
and bring him/her safely to your promised land.

We ask this through Christ our Lord.

R̷. Amen.

15 A baptized child

Lord, in our grief we call upon your mercy:
open your ears to our prayers,
and one day unite us again with N.,
who, we firmly trust,
already enjoys eternal life in your kingdom.

We ask this through Christ our Lord.

R̷. Amen.

16   A baptized child

To you, O Lord,
we humbly entrust this child,
so precious in your sight.
Take him/her into your arms
and welcome him/her into paradise,
where there will be no sorrow, no weeping nor pain,
but the fullness of peace and joy
with your Son and the Holy Spirit
for ever and ever.

    R⁊. **Amen.**

17   A young person

Lord,
your wisdom governs the length of our days.
We mourn the loss of N.,
whose life has passed so quickly,
and we entrust him/her to your mercy.
Welcome him/her into your heavenly dwelling
and grant him/her the happiness of everlasting
   youth.

We ask this through Christ our Lord.

    R⁊. **Amen.**

18   A young person

Lord God,
source and destiny of our lives,
in your loving providence
you gave us N.
to grow in wisdom, age, and grace.
Now you have called him/her to yourself.

As we grieve the loss of one so young,
we seek to understand your purpose.

Draw him/her to yourself
and give him/her full stature in Christ.
May he/she stand with all the angels and saints,
who know your love and praise your saving will.

We ask this through Christ our Lord.

℟. **Amen.**

19 Parents

Lord God, who commanded us to honor father
and mother,
look kindly upon your servants N. and N.,
have mercy upon them
and let us see them again in eternal light.

We ask this through Christ our Lord.

℟. **Amen.**

20 A parent

God of our ancestors in faith,
by the covenant made on Mount Sinai
you taught your people to strengthen the bonds
of family
through faith, honor, and love.
Look kindly upon N.,
a father/mother who sought to bind his/her
children to you.
Bring him/her one day to our heavenly home
where the saints dwell in blessedness and peace.

We ask this through Christ our Lord.

℟. **Amen.**

21 A married couple

**Lord God, whose covenant is everlasting,
have mercy upon the sins of your servants N. and N.;
as their love for each other united them on earth,
so let your love join them together in heaven.**

We ask this through Christ our Lord.

R℣. **Amen.**

22 A married couple

**Eternal Father,
in the beginning you established the love of man
  and woman
as a sign of creation.
Your own Son loves the Church as a spouse.
Grant mercy and peace to N. and N. who,
by their love for each other,
were signs of the creative love
which binds the Church to Christ.**

We ask this through Christ our Lord.

R℣. **Amen.**

23 A married couple

**Lord God,
giver of all that is true and lovely and gracious,
you created in marriage a sign of your covenant.
Look with mercy upon N. and N.
You blessed them in their companionship,
and in their joys and sorrows you bound them
  together.
Lead them into eternal peace,
and bring them to the table**

where the saints feast together in your heavenly
   home.
We ask this through Christ our Lord.

   ℞. **Amen.**

24   A wife

Eternal God,
you made the union of man and woman
a sign of the bond between Christ and the Church.

Grant mercy and peace to N.,
who was united in love with her husband.
May the care and devotion of her life on earth
find a lasting reward in heaven.
Look kindly on her husband and family/children
as now they turn to your compassion and love.
Strengthen their faith and lighten their loss.
We ask this through Christ our Lord.

   ℞. **Amen.**

25   A husband

Eternal God,
you made the union of man and woman
a sign of the bond between Christ and the Church.

Grant mercy and peace to N.,
who was united in love with his wife.
May the care and devotion of his life on earth
find a lasting reward in heaven.
Look kindly on his wife and family/children
as now they turn to your compassion and love.
Strengthen their faith and lighten their loss.
We ask this through Christ our Lord.

   ℞. **Amen.**

26 A deceased non-Christian married to a Catholic

Almighty and faithful Creator,
all things are of your making,
all people are shaped in your image.
We now entrust the soul of N. to your goodness.
In your infinite wisdom and power,
work in him/her your merciful purpose,
known to you alone from the beginning of time.
Console the hearts of those who love him/her
in the hope that all who trust in you
will find peace and rest in your kingdom.

We ask this through Christ our Lord.

℟. **Amen.**

27 An elderly person

God of endless ages,
from one generation to the next
you have been our refuge and strength.
Before the mountains were born
or the earth came to be,
you are God.
Have mercy now on your servant N.
whose long life was spent in your service.
Give him/her a place in your kingdom.
where hope is firm for all who love
and rest is sure for all who serve.

We ask this through Christ our Lord.

℟. **Amen.**

28   An elderly person

God of mercy,
look kindly on your servant N.
who has set down the burden of his/her years.
As he/she served you faithfully throughout his/her
    life,
may you give him/her the fullness of your peace
    and joy.
We give thanks for the long life of N.,
now caught up in your eternal love.
We make our prayer in the name of Jesus who is
    our risen Lord
now and for ever.

R̶. Amen.

29   One who died after a long illness

God of deliverance,
you called our brother/sister N.
to serve you in weakness and pain,
and gave him/her the grace of sharing the cross of
    your Son.
Reward his/her patience and forbearance,
and grant him/her the fullness of Christ's victory.

We ask this through Christ our Lord.

R̶. Amen.

30   One who died after a long illness

Most faithful God,
lively is the courage of those who hope in you.
Your servant N. **suffered greatly**
but placed his/her trust in your mercy.
Confident that the petition of those who mourn
pierces the clouds and finds an answer,
we beg you, give rest to N.
Do not remember his/her sins
but look upon his/her sufferings
and grant him/her refreshment, light, and peace.

We ask this through Christ our Lord.

℟. **Amen.**

31   One who died after a long illness

O God,
you are water for our thirst
and manna in our desert.
We praise you for the life of N.
and bless your mercy
that has brought his/her suffering to an end.
Now we beg that same endless mercy
to raise him/her to new life.
Nourished by the food and drink of heaven.
may he/she rest for ever
in the joy of Christ our Lord.

℟. **Amen.**

32   One who died suddenly

Lord,
as we mourn the sudden death of our brother/sister,
show us the immense power of your goodness

and strengthen our belief
that N. has entered into your presence.

We ask this through Christ our Lord.

℞. Amen.

33   One who died accidentally or violently

Lord our God,
you are always faithful and quick to show mercy.
Our brother/sister N.
was suddenly [and violently] taken from us.
Come swiftly to his/her aid,
have mercy on him/her,
and comfort his/her family and friends
by the power and protection of the cross.

We ask this through Christ our Lord.

℞. Amen.

34   One who died by suicide

God, lover of souls,
you hold dear what you have made
and spare all things, for they are yours.
Look gently on your servant N.,
and by the blood of the cross
forgive his/her sins and failings.

Remember the faith of those who mourn
and satisfy their longing for that day
when all will be made new again
in Christ, our risen Lord,
who lives and reigns with you for ever and ever.

℞. Amen.

35 One who died by suicide

Almighty God and Father of all,
you strengthen us by the mystery of the cross
and with the sacrament of your Son's resurrection.
Have mercy on our brother/sister N.
Forgive all his/her sins and grant him/her peace.
May we who mourn this sudden death be comforted
  and consoled by your power and protection.

We ask this through Christ our Lord.

  ℟. **Amen.**

36 Several persons

O Lord,
you gave new life to N. and N.
in the waters of baptism;
show mercy to them now,
and bring them to the happiness of life in your
  kingdom.

We ask this through Christ our Lord.

  ℟. **Amen.**

37 Several persons

All-powerful God,
whose mercy is never withheld
from those who call upon you in hope,
look kindly on your servants N. and N.,
who departed this life confessing your name,
and number them among your saints for evermore.

We ask this through Christ our Lord.

  ℟. **Amen.**

PRAYERS FOR THE MOURNERS

108 The following prayers for the mourners may be used in the various rites of Chapters five and six. The prayers should be chosen taking the character of the text into account as well as the place in the rite where it will occur.

1 General

**Father of mercies and God of all consolation,
you pursue us with untiring love
and dispel the shadow of death
with the bright dawn of life.**

**[Comfort your family in their loss and sorrow.
Be our refuge and our strength, O Lord,
and lift us from the depths of grief
into the peace and light of your presence.]**

**Your Son, our Lord Jesus Christ,
by dying has destroyed our death,
and by rising, restored our life.
Enable us therefore to press on toward him,
so that, after our earthly course is run,
he may reunite us with those we love,
when every tear will be wiped away.**

We ask this through Christ our Lord.

Ȓ. Amen.

2   General

Lord Jesus, our Redeemer,
you willingly gave yourself up to death,
so that all might be saved and pass from death to life.
We humbly ask you to comfort your servants in
  their grief
and to receive N. into the arms of your mercy.
You alone are the Holy One,
you are mercy itself;
by dying you unlocked the gates of life
  for those who believe in you.
Forgive N. his/her sins,
and grant him/her a place of happiness, light,
  and peace
in the kingdom of your glory for ever and ever.

    R̸. Amen.

3   General

God, all-compassionate,
ruler of the living and the dead,
you know beforehand
those whose faithful lives reveal them as your own.
We pray for those who belong to this present world
and for those who have passed to the world to come:
grant them pardon for all their sins.
We ask you graciously to hear our prayer
through the intercession of all the saints
and for your mercy's sake.

For you are God, for ever and ever.

    R̸. Amen.

4   General

Lord our God,
the death of our brother/sister N.
recalls our human condition
and the brevity of our lives on earth.
But for those who believe in your love
death is not the end,
nor does it destroy the bonds
that you forge in our lives.
We share the faith of your Son's disciples
and the hope of the children of God.
Bring the light of Christ's resurrection
to this time of testing and pain
as we pray for N. and for those who love him/her,
through Christ our Lord.

℟. Amen.

5   General

Lord God,
you are attentive to the voice of our pleading.
Let us find in your Son
comfort in our sadness,
certainty in our doubt,
and courage to live through this hour.
Make our faith strong
through Christ our Lord.

℟. Amen.

6   General

Lord,
N. is gone now from this earthly dwelling
and has left behind those who mourn his/her
absence.
Grant that as we grieve for our brother/sister
we may hold his/her memory dear
and live in hope of the eternal kingdom
where you will bring us together again.

We ask this through Christ our Lord.

℟. **Amen.**

7   General

Most merciful God,
whose wisdom is beyond our understanding,
surround the family of N. with your love,
that they may not be overwhelmed by their loss,
but have confidence in your goodness,
and strength to meet the days to come.

We ask this through Christ our Lord.

℟. **Amen.**

8   A baptized child

Lord of all gentleness,
surround us with your care
and comfort us in our sorrow,
for we grieve at the loss of this [little] child.

As you washed N. in the waters of baptism
and welcomed him/her into the life of heaven,
so call us one day

to be united with him/her
and share for ever the joy of your kingdom.

We ask this through Christ our Lord.

℞. **Amen.**

9   A baptized child

Eternal Father,
through the intercession of Mary,
who bore your Son and stood by the cross as he died,
grant to these parents in their grief
the assistance of her presence,
the comfort of her faith,
and the reward of her prayers.

We ask this through Christ our Lord.

℞. **Amen.**

10   A baptized child

Lord God,
source and destiny of our lives,
in your loving providence
you gave us N.
to grow in wisdom, age, and grace.
Now you have called him/her to yourself.

We grieve over the loss of one so young
and struggle to understand your purpose.

Draw him/her to yourself
and give him/her full stature in Christ.
May he/she stand with all the angels and saints,
who know your love and praise your saving will.

We ask this through Jesus Christ, our Lord.

℞. **Amen.**

11 A baptized child

Merciful Lord,
whose wisdom is beyond human understanding,
you adopted N. as your own in baptism
and have taken him/her to yourself
even as he/she stood on the threshold of life.
Listen to our prayers and extend to us your grace,
that one day we may share eternal life with N.,
for we firmly believe that he/she now rests with you.

We ask this through Christ our Lord.

℟. **Amen.**

12 A baptized child

Lord God,
from whom human sadness is never hidden,
you know the burden of grief
that we feel at the loss of this child.

As we mourn his/her passing from this life,
comfort us with the knowledge
that N. lives now in your loving embrace.

We ask this through Christ our Lord.

℟. **Amen.**

13 A child who died before baptism

O Lord, whose ways are beyond understanding,
listen to the prayers of your faithful people:
that those weighed down by grief
at the loss of this [little] child
may find reassurance in your infinite goodness.

We ask this through Christ our Lord.

℟. **Amen.**

14   A child who died before baptism

God of all consolation,
searcher of mind and heart,
the faith of these parents [N. and N.] is known
  to you.

Comfort them with the knowledge
that the child for whom they grieve
is entrusted now to your loving care.

We ask this through Christ our Lord.

  ℞. **Amen.**

15   A stillborn child

Lord God,
ever caring and gentle,
we commit to your love this little one,
quickened to life for so short a time.
Enfold him/her in eternal life.

We pray for his/her parents
who are saddened by the loss of their child.
Give them courage
and help them in their pain and grief.
May they all meet one day
in the joy and peace of your kingdom.

We ask this through Christ our Lord.

  ℞. **Amen.**

BIBLICAL INDEX